*"100 Easy Healthy Habits is a wonderful resource!
Tara Rayburn expertly fleshes out
what I have taught for years—-that like all success,
health is what you do every day; health is a habit.
I have seen the results in friends who've applied Tara's
healthy habits and they are amazing!
Read this book, begin this simple process and
transform the health of your mind, body and soul."*

-Jack Canfield

Coauthor of the New York Times bestselling Chicken Soup for the Soul series

100 ~Easy HEALTHY HABITS

Uplifting Habits for The Mind, Body and Soul

Tara Rayburn

The Healthy Habit Coach

LSP

LIFE SCIENCE PUBLISHING™

YESTERDAY'S WISDOM, TODAY'S DISCOVERY

To order additional copies of this book call (800) 336-6308 or visit us on the web at
lifesciencepublishers.com

ISBN
978-0-9845959-7-6
Printed in the United States of America
10 9 8 7 6 5 4 3 2

Tara Rayburn
The Healthy Habit Coach
TheHealthyHabitCoach.com
100EasyHealthyHabits.com
Tara@theHealthyHabitCoach.com

Cover Design by Tara Rayburn, Aimee Lucero
Graphic Design by Aimee Lucero, ee.lu design
Photography by Tara Rayburn
About the Author Photograph by Joey Tichenor Photography
Editing by Helen Lavine and Kim Caro

For More Information or to Book a Speaking Engagement:
Tara Rayburn, The Healthy Habit Coach – Tara@theHealthyHabitCoach.com

To order 100 Easy Healthy Habits Audio Coaching Series or Books contact
Life Science Publishing at 1-800-336-6308 or www.Lifesciencepublishers.com

A portion of sales goes to Verve Church in Las Vegas – vivalaverve.org

Thank you for Being a Ripple of Health in our World!

100EasyHealthyHabits.com

LIFE SCIENCE PUBLISHING™
YESTERDAY'S WISDOM; TODAY'S DISCOVERY

100 Easy Healthy Habits Menu

Dedication   **1**

Introduction - Removing the Mask   **3**

Healthy Habits for Life   8

Habits 1 - 25

1. Simply Start, Start Simply   9
2. Manage Your Bucket   12
3. Nutrient Rich Anchors and Safety Nets   15
4. Be Probiotic   19
5. Make a Pantry Raid   22
6. Dial in Nutrient Rich Foods   24
7. Stock with Stocks   26
8. Digestion Suggestions   29
9. Eat REAL Food   31
10. Ear Health & Happiness   33
11. Diagnostic Debate   36
12. Water Bottles   38
13. Water Wisdom   40
14. Life Breathing = Breathing Life   43
15. Nasal Hygiene - The Nose Knows!   45
16. Salt Scrubbing   47
17. Creating a Cleaner Greener Home   49
18. Personal Care Product Purification   52
19. Best Source Challenge   54
20. Fasting   56
21. Exercise as a Habit   58
22. Epsom Salt Soaks   61
23. Chew, Chew, Chew   63
24. Oilination   65
25. Make Your Own Veggie Wash   67

Habits 26 - 50

26. Teach Don't Preach   73
27. Waking Well   76
28. Get Un-Plugged!   79
29. Release, Rest and Rejuvenate   82
30. Engage the Whole Family   88
31. Eat, Sleep, Drink - Ms. Mary's Mantra   91
32. The Power of Anchors   93
33. Create Healthy Rewards   97
34. Get Curious - Listen to 3's   99
35. Grow and Practice Your Faith   101
36. Grace   103
37. Have Healthy Boundaries   105
38. Build Your Resource Base   107
39. Become the "Worker Bee"   110
40. Encourage Others   112
41. Be True to Your Quest   114
42. Build a Support System   117
43. The Cleanse   119
44. Conscious Posture   122
45. Walk the Talk   125
46. Create Healthy Traditions   127
47. Be Wise With Your Time   129
48. Focus on the Shoot   132
49. No Stress Eating   134
50. The Message of The Massage   136

Habits 51 - 75

51. Start Strong 141
52. Pre-Travel Habits 143
53. Knock out the Worst First! 145
54. Healthy Anchors Checklist 147
55. Essential Oil Checklist 150
56. Know Your Challenges 152
57. Do Your Homework - Preparation Saves Perspiration 154
58. Pack In Power 157
59. Travel Exercise - Travelcise 159
60. Make the Quart Count 161
61. Car Traveling Tips 163
62. Build In Downtime on The Road 165
63. Sinus Awareness 167
64. Hotel Hygiene 171
65. Healthy Requests 173
66. Invest in Massages, Steams or Saunas 175
67. Be Present While Away 177
68. Business as Usual? 180
69. Make Your Beverages Count 183
70. Post-Travel Habits 186
71. Don't Bring Home Hitchhikers 189
72. Build in Recovery Day 191
73. Vary Vacation's Vocation 193
74. Book Your Next Vacation Soon 195
75. Invest in Your Peaceful Return 197

Healthy Habits for Community   200
      Habits 76 - 100

76. Teach Them To Fish   202
77. Share Healthy Habits - Be the Ripple!   205
78. Make a Pot-o-Soup   208
79. Natural Breath Fresheners   210
80. Presentation is Key   214
81. Accountability Responsibility   217
82. Host a Soup Swap   219
83. Change a Habit, Change a Life   221
84. Make Your Own Personal Care Products - Together   223
85. Host a Movie Showing   225
86. Community Unity Potlucks   227
87. Keep Health Within Reach   229
88. Be Aromatic   231
89. What to Do When You Don't Know What to Do   234
90. Have an Attitude of Gratitude   236
91. Reclaim and Recycle Your Relationships   238
92. Live Off Balance On Purpose   241
93. Create A Mastermind Group   243
94. See What Isn't There - Mike Rayburn   246
95. Social Ministry vs. Social Media   249
96. Envision REAL Health   251
97. Forgive to Live   253
98. Be a Fred - Mark Sanborn   255
99. Give Gifts of Health   257
100. Be the Ripple!   259

Resources for Life   261
Gratitude   275
About the Author   278

Dedicated to

Pearl Koplinski
1911- 2006

My Pearl of Wisdom

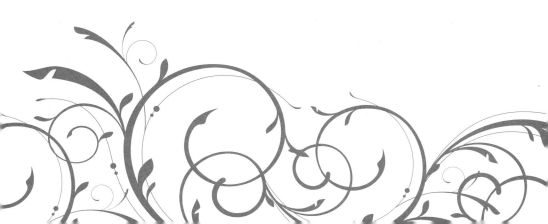

Introduction
Removing the Mask

The intention of 100 Easy Healthy Habits is to share uplifting, sustainable habits for the mind, body and soul. This project waited 5 years to be shared with you at just the right time. The birthing process really started for over 40 years ago. I am not a doctor, nutritionist or a licensed healthcare provider, nor do I aspire to be. I am a woman on a grand journey alongside my family, friends and community towards a healthier quality of life. This journey is full of amazing and confounding events, mysterious symptoms, unanswered questions, as well as answers, simple tools and old world wisdom. I have come to realize that the challenges in life we experience offer great blessings for us if we are patient and willing to accept them. This book has been such an exercise for me.

Through my family's health challenges, I have encountered some of the world's greatest "healers" and been gifted with precious wisdom. Although you may not realize this, the old world ways and wisdom still stand the test of time. The advice of parents, grandparents and our elders held keys to longevity and quality of life. Learning to weave these principles into our current lifestyle is my area of passion and expertise. 100 Easy Healthy Habits will outline "what, why and how to" for you. You will also find resources for you to dig deeper into habits and continue raising the bar for your health.

Now, about "removing the mask…" I have become increasingly aware of the challenges of teaching health, wellness and success. First, is an assumption that since I am teaching it, I must be perfect. I teach what I most need to learn. I confess, here, now, publicly, I am SO not perfect, but am loved by my creator perfectly. My role as The Healthy Habit Coach has been born from much pain, illness and adversity. I have survived abuse, struggled with eating disorders as a young adult, suffered alcohol addiction and depression much of my life. My children were born with multiple severe allergies and although blessed, my life is not without it's fair share of challenges now.

Secondly, since I am human and therefore not perfect, it is very difficult to air one's "humanity" in public. Whether a professional speaker, author or blogger, life has its challenges and will sometimes take it's toll. I am no exception, however I will continue to challenge myself by keeping it real and sharing the experiences with you along the journey. I won't judge you on yours, please be respectful of mine and others on the journey as well. We are alongside each other on this grand journey and can uplift others as we continue the quest.

I declare the mask is therefore removed permanently. Ahhh, that felt good :- D   I will not expect you to be perfect, if you remember that I am not either, nor are my families or friends. There was only one perfect life that ever existed on this planet. I'm pretty sure He did not blog…although He did author a bestseller ;-) On that note, my faith continues to be an integral part of the healing journey. Whether or not we share the same belief, please allow the wisdom of the Healthy Habit shared to surface and bring it's intention to benefit your life without judgement or concern.

By keeping an open heart and mind we all benefit. Looking at the wisdom of prior generations and valuing the principles practiced is a precious map for our journey. The Weston A. Price Foundation has been a great tool for me and I continue to support them as a Chapter Leader and carrier of the REAL food message. Gary and Mary Young, of Young Living Essential Oils have also been a tremendous resource of information and uplifting health products for our family for over 8 years.

I believe that disease doesn't just sneak up or magically appear one day. I think real health can be built or broken more by our routine choices and our daily habits than anything synthetic or contrived. How we wake, the thoughts we focus our attention on, foods we choose or don't choose, the physical activity we do, or do not choose to do – These all contribute to our well being.

It's important to point out here that our daily habits can also have a dramatic effect on the lives around us whether or not we are married, single, have children or not. You can create ripples of health in the lives around you and in our world simply by practicing healthy daily habits.

How to Use 100 Easy Healthy Habits: This book was written like a daily devotional. Open to a page, read and go! There are however, key principles covered in Section 1 – Healthy Habits for Life. This section is helpful to read first, but not necessary. There is also more detailed information in the Audio Coaching Series 100 Easy Healthy Habits which is not just the book read aloud, but a more in depth look at each habit with examples and explanations. It's almost 8 hours of Healthy Habits 101.

Here's how to best use this book:

1. Start with reading this Introduction
2. Read #1 – Simply Start and Start Simply
3. List Your Top Three Health Challenges/Goals
4. Choose one challenge/Goal to begin practicing
5. Use the Healthy Habits in this book to brainstorm habits support this goal/challenge.
6. Choose a Habit. Practice it for a week. Keep it or lose it. Repeat.

100 Easy Healthy Habits isn't meant to be a comprehensive look into every diet or health practice. Think of this as a spring board into adding and creating better, uplifting and sustainable habits. The most important task here is to start. It really doesn't matter where. Please don't over think the habit. Open the book, choose one habit, practice it for one week, review, keep it or lose it and then choose a new habit. Simple.

Even if you only adopt one habit a month, one habit a month equals 12 for the year. I have seen lives and communities transform by just practicing something as simple as making homemade chicken broth. Imagine what could happen with 12 for the year!

Peace and Be Well,

Tara Rayburn
The Healthy Habit Coach

Who Am I?

I am YOUR constant companion

I am your GREATEST helper or your HEAVIEST burden

I can push you ONWARD or drag you down

I am at YOUR command

Those who are GREAT – I have made great

Those who are failures – I have made FAILURES

YOU may run me for profit or run me for ruin…
makes no difference to ME

Take me, Train me, be FIRM with me, and I will lay the
WORLD at your feet

Be EASY with me and I will DESTROY you

WHO AM I ?

- anonymous

I'M YOUR DAILY HABITS

Healthy Habits for Life

Introduction

Although this book is intended to be read in any order, the Healthy Habits for Life section does explain some basic foundations and might be helpful to read first. Each habit throughout the book will list resources and reference other habits covered in 100 Easy Healthy Habits. Each habit in this book could be and in many cases is a complete book or collection of books by various authors. My intention is to give you the basics of a particular habit and a list of further resources for you to dig in deeper.

Remember, that it really isn't important where you start, the most important action is to Start. Healthy Habit #1 Simply Start is a good launch into how to choose a habit. Other habits in this section are important concepts and foundations for sustainable health. Listen to 100 Easy Healthy Habits audio coaching series to learn more, enhance these concepts and solidify their meanings.

Keep in mind, none of us are perfect. I certainly am not. I'm on the journey too. I have many of the same struggles as you do. I use these habits to get myself back on track quickly and to raise the bar where ever I am. I also believe that there are no perfect diets, no perfect exercises or magic pills to create REAL health. REAL health is earned through our daily habits. What we do daily and how we eat, sleep and think all can uplift our health… or not. One habit can forever change the course of your life. 100 Easy Healthy Habits is intended for you to start adding habits at your own pace, in order to uplift your mind, body and soul and become a Ripple of Health in our world.

Habit 1

Simply Start, Start Simply

Steps for Starting a Healthy Habit

1. **Simply Decide:** The first step is to "decide" to change a habit. This doesn't mean you have to "quit" anything. Most people find it easier to add a habit rather than give one up.

2. **Make a List:** Next, make a prioritized list of three to five of your top health goals or challenges.

3. **Choose One Goal:** Choose one goal as a starting place. Don't overthink this. It could be your top priority goal or a smaller, easier goal to get the process started. The point is simply to take that first step in the right direction and set yourself up for success.

4. **Brainstorm 10-20 Habits:** Next, take out some paper and brainstorm 10-20 habits you could begin that would support this goal/challenge. Nothing is too crazy, small or too simple. Let the creativity flow and enlist the help of others for ideas.

Skim this book or listen to the audio series to get some great starter habits.

5. **Pick One Habit:** Time to choose one habit to start with from your list. Make sure it is one that is reasonable for you to do. Be honest with yourself and set yourself up for success.

6. **Just Do it!** Embrace and practice that habit wholeheartedly for at least one week. Do whatever it takes to make it happen for the week. Journaling is a great way to track the effects of your changes.

7. **Evaluate:** After one week decide if your habit made a difference. Is it worth continuing or not? Does it need tweaking? Did you feel better, worse, the same? Either keep it or move on to the next habit from your list. Again, don't overthink this. The most important idea here is the actual process of creating a sustainable, new habit.

8. **Repeat Process:** Choose a new habit to test out and repeat process as often as is comfortable for your success. Start it… Stick with it… and Anchor it! Habits can be added, released, rotated and tweaked as often as you see fit. If you are working with dietary habits, it may take 2-3 weeks to feel the benefit of the change.

I have seen one habit by one person change many lives. Now imagine if you add/change just one habit a month. That is 12 Healthy Habits for the year! If just one can transform your life and the lives around you, imagine what 12 could do!

Others will begin to notice a change in you. It may be subtle or obvious, but they'll start to see it and ask you what are you doing differently. Don't be shy, share it with them. Encourage them to start.

> **NOTE:** A powerful tool for your success is anchoring positive associations with the reward of this process and its effects on your mind, body and spirit.

Related Healthy Habits:
- #32 The Power of Anchors
- #1-100 ;-)

Resources:

100 Easy Healthy Habits: Uplifting Habits for the Mind, Body and Soul – Audio coaching series and book by Tara Rayburn

The Healthy Habit Coach Resources -
- Blog – thehealthyhabitcoach.com/blog
- LinkedIn – linkedin.com/in/tararayburn
- Twitter – twitter.com/TaraRayburn
- Facebook – facebook.com/thehealthyhabitcoach
- Google+ – plus.google.com - Tara Rayburn
- Pinterest – pinterest.com/tararayburn
- Instagram – instagram.com/healthyhabits
- The OGG Blog – Of God's Grace – ofgodsgrace.blogspot. com

Manage Your Bucket

The Best Health Care is to Care for Your Health

What:

Our body is a grand vessel or a wonderful bucket. Our vessel starts off pretty clean and clear, but over time burdensome elements can fill it up and wear it out faster than we can cleanse it. Regardless of how "full" you may think your bucket is, the amount of physical, emotional and spiritual bombardments we are exposed to daily are far greater than even five years ago. It is widely documented that the amount of chemicals our children are exposed to on a daily basis is greater than what our grandparents were exposed to throughout their whole lifetime. This knowledge, coupled with the fact that our lifestyles don't lend themselves to cleansing faster than we are "filling up," creates an environment of "toxicity" which can lead to a whole host of symptoms and potential chronic issues.

Why:

Our immune systems have more challenges than ever before, which means being proactive by "managing our bucket" is how we can stay ahead of the curve and create REAL longterm health. Managing means just that. There are many factors in our world that we cannot control, so becoming experts on ways to empty our buckets is a great way to start stacking the odds in our favor. Daily stressors of all kinds will always exist, so practicing daily stress relief or ongoing cleansing habits will help us by focusing on caring for our health.

How To:

Think of your body as a bank account. If you have been withdrawing more than you have been depositing, you'll eventually go broke. If you have been doing things that wear your body, mind and soul down, then start dialing in the things that enrich and uplift your system. This WHOLE book is just full of Healthy Habits for you to start!

Here are some Simple, FREE or Inexpensive Ideas:
- 15 minute Power rests – Healthy Habit #29 Release, Rest & Rejuvenate
- Salt Scrubs – Healthy Habit #16 Salt Scrubbing
- Cleansing Baths – Healthy Habit #22 Epsom Salt Soaks
- Drink & Eat from clean, green containers – Healthy Habit #12 Water Bottles
- Take an Electronics Fast – Healthy Habit #20 Fasting
- Sit or Walk outside, in direct sunlight for at least 15 minutes
- Mindful Meals – Healthy Habits #8 Digestion Suggestions, #23 Chew, Chew, Chew
- Daily Oilinations – Healthy Habit – #24 Oilination

Related Healthy Habits:

- #20 Fasting
- #43 The Cleanse
- #1-100 ;-)

Resources:

- 100 Easy Healthy Habits: Uplifting Habits for the Mind, Body and Soul – Audio coaching series and book by Tara Rayburn
- The Healthy Habit Coach Blog – thehealthyhabitcoach. com/blog
- **The Complete Master Cleanse** by Tom Woloshyn – themastercleanse.org
- Environmental Working Group – ewg.org
- **How to Feel 10 Years Younger in 90 days or Less** by Dr. Pete Hilgartner, www.hilgartnerhealth.com
- **Healthy Healing** by Linda Page, Ph.D

Habit 3

Nutrient Rich Anchors and Safety Nets

Practice the 80:20 Rule. If your anchors are in place at least 80% of the time, then your baseline health stays strong.

What:

Nutrient rich anchors are foods, beverages, supplements, etc. that are a mainstay in your health regimen. These occur more often then not and carry a big "bang for the buck" benefit for you. For example, my family relies on organic, non-GMO, homemade meals and real/whole food based supplements, digestive enzymes and fermented cod liver oil. While sleep isn't a "nutritional" anchor, it can really affect your health and the absorption of nutrients. It's a big player in our house.

Safety Nets are those items you keep on hand to boost your system when you are starting to feel run down or simply know you need to catch up. My family dials in massages, bone broths, soups, essential oils and herbal teas for great boosts.

Why:

Even if you do eat well, we all get busy and slide sometimes. If our daily anchors are in place, we are much more resistant to viruses, stress and random hits like infections and even injuries. Follow the 80:20 rule. If your anchors are in place at least 80% of the time, then your baseline health stays strong. However, if you already have a compromised immune system, then shoot for 90%. This might seem hard, but it is still better than ending up symptomatic, in bed or worse. Time and energy invested in staying well pays off exponentially.

Keep "Safety Nets" on hand to use as soon as you know you are not "managing your bucket" well or as soon as you start getting that rundown feeling. The longer you wait, the more it takes to feel well. There is no guarantee, and by law I cannot tell you that you won't get ill. But just ask yourself, "Doesn't it make sense to eat, drink or use something to help your body do its job rather than something that is going to burden your body more with side effects?" Remember, the "Best Health Care System is to Care for Your Health!"

How To:

The key is that these anchors work for your lifestyle and give a big boost for your family's system. Be realistic and specific for your needs. Keep some basics in your diet daily via food, beverages or whole food supplements. Get a natural resource book, search holistic blogs, enlist the help of a Healthy Habit Coach or other Integrative Health Professionals.

Here is a shortlist of my family's anchors:
- Bone Broths – for quick soups or cooking quinoa or sprouted rice
- Digestive Enzyme support for adults and kids.
- Peppermint Essential Oil supports digestion and eases an upset tummy.
- Probiotics every night or in our diet daily
- Supplements made from REAL food daily (ie: Juice Plus+, Young Living)
- Clean, filtered water
- Greens (dandelions, swiss chard, kale, spinach) chop & add to meals
- Get enough rest and sleep.
- Fermented Cod Liver Oil daily
- Avoid sugar, empty starches and non-nutritional snacks

TIPS & TRICKS:
Anchors & Safety Nets can also be practices like getting enough sleep, daily exercise or stress releasing techniques.

Related Habits:
- #6 Dial in Nutrients
- #9 Eat REAL Food

Resources:
- Weston A. Price Foundation – westonaprice.org
- Price-Pottenger Nutrition Foundation – ppnf.org
- Dr. Joseph Mercola Blog – mercola.com
- **Essential Gluten-Free Recipes 2nd Edition** by Tara

Rayburn and Mary Vars – lifesciencepublishers.com or Amazon.com

- **Nourishing Traditions** by Sally Fallon Morrell and Mary Enig
- Juice Plus+ supplements – thehealthyhabitcoach.com/store
- Young Living – Therapeutic Grade Essential Oils , Quality personal care products and Diffusers – YoungLiving.com *Note: if you already work with a Young Living Distributor, please honor that relationship for ordering. If you are not currently working with a distributor or you are interested in becoming one, please see my website or see Resources in the back of the book.
- Fermented Cod Liver Oil – Green Pasture – greenpasture.org

Habit 4

Be Probiotic

In my opinion, the importance of "The Critter Factor" in establishing a strong immune system and greater quality of life is perhaps one of the most overlooked elements in our world.

What:

You have beneficial flora (probiotic) and unbeneficial flora (pathogens, viruses, bacteria, parasites, etc.) that co-exist in your body at any given time. Most traditional cultures' natural diets had ways to balance this inner ecosystem. For instance, they soaked grains and naturally fermented foods and beverages. This process increases "digest-ability" and adds pre-biotics and probiotics. Pre-biotics are foods that feed the beneficial flora in the body. Unfortunately, the SAD (Standard American Diet) of highly processed foods, preservatives and sugar tends to feed the unbeneficial flora in our bodies instead. The fact is, that we as a culture, and as a world are rapidly losing the wisdom, practices, and thus the "battle" of a healthy, balanced inner ecosystem.

Why:

Yeasts and other pathogens have toxins they release into our bodies and, if left unchecked, will literally pollute our bodies. These "mycotoxins" being released into our bodies are being linked to many health problems and chronic issues. The use of antibiotics, even when there is suspicion of viral or other issues, is a dangerous blanket treatment offsetting our inner ecosystem even more. Whether you take antibiotics or not, they are beginning to contaminate our water, food supply and our bodies.

Beneficial flora needs to be fed and replaced daily since there are so many factors killing them off (rampant use of antibiotics, environmental/household toxins, poor nutrition, poor water and stress). Since the forces against these probiotic allies are strong, we must be proactive about replenishing them and keeping a balance in our bodies. This delicate balance of our inner ecosystem determines the strength of our immune system.

How To:

GOOD: Find a balanced Probiotic supplement. If you do not tolerate dairy make sure to find one that is non-dairy. (see resources)

BETTER: Rotate your probiotics every so often. There are many strains of probiotics. Even too much of a good thing can be too much.

BEST: Dial in foods and beverages throughout the day like Kombucha, Kefir (milk, coconut, or even water kefir), Kim Chi, cultured veggies like beets, salads and sauerkrauts. It is great to take a dose of a probiotic source just before bedtime. The body heals at night and supplying it with powerful inner ecosystem "critters" aids in that healing.

My family's habit: Although we dial in probiotic foods and beverages, we also add supplements at bedtime too for extra support. I'll add a probiotic powder to a little shot glass of coconut water kefir.

Resources:

- Dr. OhHira's Probiotics
- PRObiotic 225 by Ortho Molecular Products
- Coconut Wate Kefir by Body Ecology, Tonix or learn to make your own (see my recipe book)
- **Nourishing Traditions Cookbook** by Sally Fallon Morrell and Mary Enig
- **Essential Gluten-Free Recipes 2nd Edition** by Tara Rayburn and Mary Vars – See Bountiful Beverage section and Resources – lifesciencepublishers.com or Amazon.com

Habit 5

Make a Pantry Raid

What:

A "Pantry Raid" is the habit of enlisting some fresh eyes to help you see the crutch foods that might be causing problems in your health. It can also be simply getting input for raising the bar on the foods you typically keep on hand.

Why:

Typically, in most homes the pantry is the first place people go to find snacks. Snacks are also the biggest place people make or break healthy dietary choices whether it's late night snacking or "freebie" mentality. People oftentimes don't even acknowledge what they are eating when they snack and don't realize the impact it may be having on their health. They only look at meal time and forget how much they might have added to their daily sugar, fat or junk intake by hitting the pantry. We call the pantry the "carb closet" or the "comfort-food cave" in our house. I can always tell when someone is rooting around in there and realize it as a big wildcard in my family's health if it's not stocked with healthy choices.

How To:

I know that my goal isn't to overwhelm or tell someone to throw everything away. For example, I will look for themes such as cooking fats/oils. Fat is your friend. To be clear, fat from clean, healthy, stable when heated, fat is your friend. Cooking fats should be stable when heated, such as coconut oil, palm oil or rendered animal fat from organic sources. Real butter, if you tolerate dairy, is best when it's from grass fed cows. (And of course will be kept in the fridge not the pantry ;-) No cooking with corn, soy, safflower or other vegetable oils. Olive oil is best used after cooking or added to salad dressings. (see Westonapricefoundation.org)

When engaging in a Pantry Raid, I'll also remind people to look at the ingredient list on packages. Whether or not you have allergies and need to read labels, sticking to the 1/2 inch or five ingredient rule is a good one. If you see a huge list of unpronounceable words, or preservatives, dyes, "code" words for MSG like "natural flavorings," then don't buy them again. We also call this the "pinky rule." If the list is longer than your pinky width, then steer clear.

Resources:

- Dr. Oz and other health oriented shows run Pantry Raid segments often.
- Chef Shane Kelly – chefshanekelly.com
- The Village Green Network is a great collection of REAL food bloggers to help you learn more about REAL food choices – villagegreennetwork.com
- **Essential Gluten-Free Recipes 2nd Edition** by Tara Rayburn and Mary Vars – See The Basics section – lifesciencepublishers. com or Amazon.com

Habit 6

Dial in Nutrient Rich Foods

What:

If you look up the terms Nutrients, Nutrition or Nourishing you can find a general consensus of substances necessary for life and growth. However, the specifics of those definitions have changed over the years. When I looked these terms up over five years ago, many of the definitions included the term "naturally occurring" substances and now I don't seem to find that definition given. Why? Well, quite frankly most people eat highly processed foods that have been depleted of naturally occurring nutrients and therefore must either be "enriched" with manmade/synthetic nutrients or simply be consumed as is…very low to no nutritional value. If you eat foods created in a lab, you'll need a lab to digest them too :-0

Man cannot make a better version of what God/Nature brings us naturally. The nutrients found in REAL food have all the co-factors needed to be properly absorbed. It is easy to become out of balance when you begin to isolate specific minerals, vitamins, etc. without also adding the complementing nutrients as well.

Why: ·

Many of the health issues in our world have a root cause of poor immune systems and compromised digestive systems. Your body is capable of amazing feats of healing when it is given the proper tools…aka. Nutrients. The solution is simple, dial in nutrient rich food!

How To:

- Add veggie purees to recipes and meals
- Include soups and stocks
- Add chopped, sliced or diced veggies to recipes
- Eat the colors of the rainbow. Different naturally occurring colors usually mean different nutrients.
- Make your beverages count with enzymes, probiotics, detoxifying elements and vitamins and minerals.

Resources:

- **The World's Healthiest Foods** by George Mateljan
- **Essential Gluten-Free Recipes 2nd Edition** by Tara Rayburn and Mary Vars – lifesciencepublishers.com or Amazon.com
- TheHealthyHomeEconomist.com
- Chef Shane Kelly – chefshanekelly.com
- Mary Vars the Mentor Mom – mkvars@verizon.com

Habit 7

Stock with Stocks

What:

Stock is a broth made from beef, chicken or fish bones. Also referred to as bone broth. They generally take anywhere from 24 to 48 hours to simmer in order to pull all the nutrients out of the bones. Although you can make stock from vegetables, it doesn't carry the same deep nutritional properties as bone broths. Chicken and fish broths are very mineral rich and more digestible than the beef broths in my opinion and a great way to nourish people who either are having difficulty keeping food down or on special diets. We have even used broth with people on feeding tubes with great success. **Note: Must clean or change tubes more often, but it is worth the effort in payoff for replenishing the nutrients in the body.

Why?

The Healing Magic of Broth
Reprinted with permission from Essential Gluten-Free Recipes by Tara Rayburn and Mary Vars

Health Benefits of Chicken Broth:

1. The ultimate, nutrient-rich, fast food!
2. Outstanding healing powers for the digestive system

3. Easily absorbed mineral source
4. High calcium content
5. Great for building strong bones and healthy joints
6. Protein sparer (you can eat less protein when you are using broths. Thank you Chef Monica Corrado for that great term.)
7. Great comfort beverage
8. Heals the gut lining (fantastic for children with autism, ADD/HD, etc.)
9. Community builder (make it together and share with others)
10. Bone broth is #1 in our family medicine cabinet for all these reasons.

How To:

The Healing Magic of Broth

Reprinted with permission from *Essential Gluten-Free Recipes"
by Tara Rayburn and Mary Vars

Chicken Broth Recipe:

2 Tablespoons of raw apple cider vinegar

One whole organic chicken cut up or two leftover carcasses

Extra chicken backs, necks, feet if you can get them (these parts have more cartilage and are full of healing gelatin)

4-5 coarsely chopped seasonal root vegetables

5 stalks of celery coarsely chopped

1 organic yellow onion coarsely chopped

3-4 cloves fresh garlic

Directions:

• Add 4-6 quarts of spring or filtered water.

• Add apple cider vinegar, chicken, root veggies and all ingredients.

- Let sit for 1/2 hour to start pulling minerals out of bones.
- Next, bring to a boil and skim brown foam from surface.
- Pull out chicken and take off the meat after about an hour of cooking to use in soup later.
- Lower to simmer for 24 hours.
- Strain and pour into clean canning jars with 1½ to 2 inches of breathing space.
- Cool, close lid and put into refrigerator until completely cooled.
- Put excess jars in freezer (must have breathing space and be cold).
- Glass jars may crack when freezing. Try glass freezer baking dishes or other freeze safe containers with lids for better success.

Optional:
Once cooled, skim fat and use it for cooking.
Chicken heads and feet offer huge nutrients to your broth. The amount of gelatin they contain is far better for your joints than any supplement. Check availability with local farmers. These optional parts can be a little alarming to some people so don't let the squeamish look in the pot.

Resources:
- **Essential Gluten-Free Recipes 2nd Edition** by Tara Rayburn and Mary Vars
- Chef Monica Corrado is a REAL Food educator and teaches amazing cooking classes – simplybeingwell.com
- **Nourishing Traditions Cookbook** by Sally Fallon Morrell and Mary Enig
- **Nourishing Broth** by Sally Fallon Morrell and Dr. Kaayla Daniel - coming in 2014! ;-)

Habit 8

Digestion Suggestions

"You are what you eat. More specifically, you are what you assimilate."

– Dr. Pete Hilgartner, Hilgartner Health Institute

What:

Digestive enzymes are essential in the absorption of the nutrients you eat. Through good sustainable farming practices, traditional food preparation and recipes, diets long ago usually contained plenty of enzymes for good absorption. Not so in today's fast-paced, convenience lifestyle.

Why?

In short, we are born with systemic enzymes, which assist the body in major functions, and digestive enzymes which help us assimilate our diet. You cannot produce any more systemic enzymes and, if your body runs out or is constantly in need of more digestive enzymes, it will rob from systemic enzymes. It robs Peter to pay Paul and will start causing cascading effects of body system disfunction. We can dramatically change this problem simply by becoming a student of supporting our digestion through simple habits, foods, beverages and stress-free mealtimes.

How To:

- Many people don't realize where digestion actually begins. Digestion actually begins when you smell the food cooking! Yes, really! If you are not cooking it, be sure to swing by and take in the aromas about ten minutes before you eat.
- Take a spoon of Raw Apple Cider Vinegar about ten minutes before eating to set your stomach up for good digestion.
- Actually sit at a table while eating and take three deep slow breaths before eating. This takes you out of the "fight or flight" mode and actually sets your body up well for good digestion.
- Bless your meal. Express gratitude for the hands that grew it and prepared it, that it may be of good use to your health and that you may be of good use for God's work ;-)
- Two drops of Di-Gize essential oil blend is a great digestive support or use another broad spectrum digestive enzyme supplement.
- Digestive supportive beverages: chicken broth, kombucha, water with lemon essential oil, coconut water kefir, herbal sun tea.

Resources:

- **Essential Gluten Free Recipes** by Tara Rayburn and Mary Vars – Dr. Pete's section on Digestive and Systemic Enzymes pages 40-44
- Digestive Enzyme Supplements – Young Living – youngliving.org/tararayburn, Enzymedica – enzymedica.com
- Digestive Beverages – *Essential Gluten Free Recipes'* Bountiful Beverage Section, Kombucha and Coconut Water kefir sold at most health food stores or learn to make your own.

Habit 9

Eat REAL Food

What:

In my opinion, REAL food is defined as naturally occurring nutrient rich foods and beverages as close to a natural state as possible. This means "low to "no" to "un" processed foods and beverages. I would also add to that definition without synthetic preservatives, colors, chemicals or other additives. My friend Dr. Pete Hilgartner says, "Eat it if it rots, just eat it before it rots." I like to restate that, Eat as many foods as possible that don't have expiration dates on them. If it actually has a shelf life, it probably has "life" to it. Avoid foods with long or unpronounceable ingredient lists on them.

Why?

People today have a huge amount of toxins bombarding their bodies daily. No one really knows how much is too much or how all these toxins will be reacting with each other inside our bodies. Many folks ask if buying organic is important and I say YES! The more important point is about buying foods that are NON Genetically Modified (Non GMO). I cannot express how much GMO foods are a wild card in our health. Nobody really knows what they are going to ultimately do to our bodies. Look at examples like seeds grown to resist weed killer or to explode the stomachs of bugs eating them – it is bound to have some effect on us. More importantly, how is food grown from seeds designed not to produce germinating seeds going to ultimately affect us? The answer is nobody really knows. Food grown not to produce life will have some effect on the lives eating that food. In the words of my friend AnnMarie Michaels (CheeseSlave), "My child is NOT a science experiment."

How To:

Eat foods labeled organic and non-GMO as much as possible if not always. Although local is important, if it isn't organic and non-GMO, it's not worth supporting those local farmers unless they are willing to change or are actually practicing the right way and just haven't gotten certified. Get to know your farmers and visit their farms if possible. The magic that happens is unbelievable. If they aren't aware of these issues, offer to educate them with good resources. They have families too, and want good health. Avoid foods with long or unpronounceable ingredient lists on them.

Resources:

- Support companies with foods labeled by the NonGMO Project – nongmoproject.org
- **Nourishing Traditions** by Sally Fallon Morrell and Mary Enig
- The Village Green Network REAL food bloggers – villagegreennetwork.com
- Chef Shane Kelly – chefshanekelly.com

Ear Health & Happiness

What:

Many adults and children today suffer with a variety of ear related issues. From excess wax build up, to chronic ear infections, to vertigo or hearing loss. I know I have suffered severe pain when descending on an airplane. While there are various reasons for these problems, many people have chosen to take antibiotics to attempt to solve them. This can cause even greater health issues, which lead to more antibiotic treatment and of course, then more health issues.

Why?

Not all earaches are created or caused equally. If antibiotics are used to treat them, your immune system is being compromised in the process. Some issues can be traced to systemic problems like body pH, food allergies, fungal overgrowth (Candida), viruses, environmental allergies or reactions to chemical exposure. None of these causes are ultimately made better at the core by antibiotics.

How To:

Fight Infection

Balance ear pH with white vinegar inside the ear OR put

lavender essential oil BEHIND the ear and two drops on a cotton ball over top (never inside the ear).

Ease ear pain

with warm olive oil.

Stave Off Chronic Ear Infections and Eczema

Do an elimination diet to test for food allergies/sensitivities. Wheat and Dairy are the biggest culprits especially if they aren't prepared properly.

Fungal issues

Do not go to bed/sleep with ears wet. Use hair dryer if necessary to keep ear dry. Follow candida diet protocol to balance yeasts in the body.

Ear Pressure during flights

Put peppermint essential oil on the boney protrusion BEHIND the ear (never inside) and over temples and sinuses (not too close to eyes) to open up sinuses and eliminate pressure pain. Lavender behind the ears is also good if you are prone to getting ear infections after air travel.

Overall Immune Support

Probiotics orally every night before bedtime. Your body heals at night, so giving it a dose of beneficial "critters" is exponentially helpful.

NOTE: Some strains of probiotics are specific to balancing yeast in the body such as saccharomyces boulardii found in certain brands. I suggest rotating brands every couple of months to build up a strong immune system.

Related Habits:

- #4 Be Probiotic

Resources:

- Read a book about Alkalizing or pH Balancing the body to get basic idea.
- **Healing Childhood Ear Infections** by Dr. Michael A. Schmidt
- Joette Calabrese for Homeopathy – joettecalabrese.com
- Young Living – Therapeutic Grade Essential Oils , Quality personal care products and Diffusers – YoungLiving.com *Note: if you already work with a Young Living Distributor, please honor that relationship for ordering. If you are not currently working with a distributor or you are interested in becoming one, please see my website or see Resources in the back of the book.
- **Healthy Healing A Guide to Self Healing** by Linda Page

Habit 11

Diagnostic Debate

Do you really have to wait for a diagnosis to start adding healthy habits now?

What:

Fact: We have a reactive medical model in our world now based on fixing what is broken rather than a proactive model rewarding uplifting sustainable habits to create longevity and a great quality of life. Many of our diagnostic measures are invasive and cause further stress on an already stressed system. Unfortunately, many of these procedures never arrive at an accurate diagnosis or don't solve the issue because the "approved" protocol never really healed the root cause of the symptoms in the first place.

IMPORTANT: I am not a doctor and I am not suggesting you don't seek an answer for your symptoms. What I am saying is: There are many ways to promote healing by adding or improving habits. The path of wellness can also be built by releasing habits/foods/beverages that do not support good, sound health. Always get your doctor's ok. The habits I'm talking about will likely be supported by your medical team. For example, cutting out sugar, walking for 20 minutes, chewing your food better, breathing more efficiently – most doctors are not going to have a problem with these habits. When in doubt, ask! Your doctor is on Your team.

Why?

Fiction: We have to wait until we receive a diagnosis in order to improve our health and the diagnosis is always right. Because of all the layers of health issues people have today and the use of suppressive medicine (with its own side effects), "mis" or "missed" diagnosis is always a possibility. Creating sustainable daily habits that support good health is a long term plan, not a short term fix.

How To:

- Choose your top 3 health issues/challenges and pick one to focus on.
- Brainstorm 10-20 habits to support that issue.
- Choose one that will be supportive to that issue.
- Ask your doctor for support.
- Go!

Related Habits:

- #1 Simply Start

Resources:

- 100 Easy Healthy Habits Audio Coaching Series and Book by Tara Rayburn
- **Healthy Healing** by Linda Page
- **Essential Oils Desk Reference** published by Life Science Publishing

Habit 12

Water Bottles

What:

What you actually drink "out" of is equally as important as "what" you are drinking. We recommend drinking from glass or stainless steel containers. Although there are plastic bottles said to be "safe" we do not use them. This really applies to what you cook in and eat out of as well.

Why?

Plastic water bottles can leach toxins into your water that can interfere with your hormones. Your hormones run your body systems. When they are interfered with and don't work right, then neither do you. Plastics also contribute to major waste in our world's landfills. These plastics then leach their toxins into the water supply system affecting our water quality and ultimately our health. Cheap metal water bottles can leach heavy metals into your system which are very difficult to detox from and are being linked to many major health issues.

How To:

Buy glass water bottles or drink from glass canning jars. They even make glass canning jar drinking glasses. You can also buy food grade quality stainless steel water bottles. Don't assume, if it looks like metal, its stainless steel. We also like adding essential oils to our water bottles. NEVER add essential oils to plastic water bottles of any kind. Oils are designed to leach out toxins which is what they will do in your water bottle. So please don't drink water with oils from plastic at all.

NOTE: I also like glass and stainless steel for my cooking.

Resources:

- Glass water and baby bottles from LifeFactory.com
- Stainless Steel water bottles – Klean Kanteen – kleankanteen. com
- Young Living Titanium Cooking Pans – youngliving.org/ tararayburn
- Glass canning jars – Mason or Kerr check online for best prices and sizes. I ordered some
- Canning Jar Drinking glasses – I ordered some from jarstore. com They came quickly and intact.
- Great cooking pans and casserole dishes – Le Creuset – cookware.lecreuset.com and Pyrex available at most kitchen stores.

Habit 13

Water Wisdom

What:

Get the best source of water you can. Water makes up the majority of our world and our bodies (over 70%). Water quality is also a hot topic of debate. Most worldwide water supplies are taking a beating from environmental and manmade toxic exposures, making it more difficult to find pure sources of water.

People debate what is best: Home filtration, spring water, alkalized water, reverse osmosis. Basically, you want water with little to no chemicals and that contains nutrients. Some people advocate drinking distilled water, but I've learned that it is a hungry water and will leach nutrients from your body. It is fine for a short term cleanse but not great for longterm health. The same goes if you are drinking reverse osmosis water. While RO has little to no chemicals and microorganisms, it also has little to no nutrients and can acidify your body as well as leach nutrients. At the time of this writing, I know they are working on RO systems that replenish the minerals in the water. Look forward to seeing their success.

So what's all the fuss about alkalized water? Going back to the pH balancing conversation (see Healthy Habit #10), the concept is that we have so much acidifying our bodies that alkalizing water can help us get back to balance. Good in theory, but not sure it holds water (yeah, I said that). If you have a machine at your sink and get the water-fresh alkalized water, then likely – yes. If you buy it and it sits in plastic containers, it will lose its alkalized state before long. These are my opinions and not scientific fact. Another argument is that if you have a good diet and health practices that you may even get too alkalized, but most people will not be in this state.

Why?

Water can replenish nutrients or deplete them. Be sure you are replenishing them so you do not adversely compromise your immune system. Your body needs water in order to function properly. Without water, it can't do its job.

How To:

- Do the best you can and bless your meals and your water.
- I know people who write positive words or statements on a piece of tape on their water bottles.
- Check out the Rice Experiment regarding Dr. Masaru Emoto's work.
- If you are able to have a whole house filtration system – great, but do your homework.
- If you drink reverse osmosis that doesn't have a way to replenish nutrients, then you must build them back in with herbs, teas and essential oils. Please don't add synthetic nutrients.
- Add herbs & essential oils to alkalize and nourish your water.
- If you buy spring water in plastic containers, the rule of thumb is the thicker the plastic, the less it leaches.

- You can also bring glass jars or glass containers to local stores specializing in quality water.

Resources:

- For the power of words and thoughts on water, check out the work of Dr. Masaru Emoto - masaru-emoto.net.
- Check out Kangen Alkaline Water Machines or Ozone systems.
- Reverse osmosis water filtration, Nikken and EcoQuest are some good companies out there.

Habit 14

Life Breathing =
Breathing Life

"Practicing regular, mindful breathing can be calming and energizing and can even help with stress-related health problems ranging from panic attacks to digestive disorders."

-Andrew Weil, M.D.

What:

Most people spend much of their lives with shoulders rolled down and a slight slump in the body. This makes it difficult to fully breathe. Years ago when I was a full time graphic designer in Nashville, (Griffon Graphix) I realized that I would periodically stop breathing throughout the day and have to suddenly gasp for air. I was so engrossed in the creative process that I literally forgot to breathe. Now that can't be good for the brain and creativity, can it?

Why?

I have learned over the years how chronic illness, grief, anger, depression all adversely affect breathing. This in turn adversely affects thinking and overall health. To properly think and to properly function we need to practice proper breathing.

How To:

- Create posture and habits that encourage deep and full breaths for circulating oxygen throughout the brain and body.
- Set a timer off periodically as a posture and air checking time.
- Learn and practice Isometrics.
- Be mindful of your breathing throughout the day.
- Yoga classes are oftentimes a good source for learning proper breathing habits.
- Nia is another great way to gently exercise and practice great breathing habits.

Resources:

- OxyCise – Deep Breathing and gentle isometrics – oxycise.com
- Breathing Exercises – drweil.com
- Nia Technique Exercise – nianow.com
- Check out my guest editor post call Sitting Well on Caldera Spas 20 Minute Renewal blog – calderaspas.com/en/health-wellness/20-minute-renewal/2013/01/24/sitting-well-improve-posture-these-10-healthy-habits/

Habit 15

Nasal Hygiene -
The Nose Knows!

What:

Many ancient cultures recognized the importance of good oxygen flow to the brain and throughout the body, and practiced good habits to strengthen their sinuses. Nowadays, there is a lot combating our breathing like poor air quality, pollens, pollutants and other chemicals which adversely affect our sinus passages. Improper diet and adulterated foods and drinks can also create inflammation and chronic mucus causing symptoms, syndromes and health issues.

Why:

Due to many of the reasons listed above, many people have issues like sleep apnea and sinusitis and cannot sleep well. This in turn creates more health problems like brain fog, poor concentration and depression. Caring for your nose is important in order to be assured you are getting a proper amount of oxygen into your brain and body for clarity and overall health.

How To:

- Neti pot – In times of high pollen or other environmental issues use a neti pot am and pm.
- Nasal swabbing – In a small glass jar mix a carrier oil with a couple of drops of essential oil (I use Purification Blend), and dip Q-Tips into the mixture and swab each nostril.
- Practice breathing exercises to clear and strengthen the sinuses.
- Cool Mist Essential Oil Diffusing is a great way to sanitize the air in your home, office or workplace. It also is a great way to support your whole family's health – pets included. Family favorites to diffuse: Purification, Raven, R.C. Blend, Lemongrass and Lemon.

Resources:

- Baraka Ceramic Net Pots – sinussupport.com
- Young Living – Therapeutic Grade Essential Oils , Quality personal care products and Diffusers – YoungLiving.com *Note: if you already work with a Young Living Distributor, please honor that relationship for ordering. If you are not currently working with a distributor or you are interested in becoming one, please see my website or see Resources in the back of the book.
- Cool Mist Diffusers – DiffuserWorld.com – For a discount code A735SAVE5
- How to Use the Neti Pot Video – BarakaNetiPots on YouTube. com
- Castor Oil from The Heritage Store – heritagestore.com or BAAR – baar.com

Salt Scrubbing

What:

Salt Scrubbing is using sea salt as a body scrub in the bath or shower with the intention of supporting the removal of toxins by your lymphatic system. This process also serves to slough off dead skin and purify the skin.

Why?

Your skin is your largest organ for detoxification. Practicing habits to slough off old skin cells, purify new ones and to support the lymphatic system in releasing toxic build up is time well invested toward health and wellness.

How To:

I like to keep a medium to small glass jar with fine sea salt in it. At some point towards the end of my shower or bath I will put sea salt in the palm of my hand and repeat small circular motions over my skin starting from my feet to torso, hands toward heart, chest toward abdomen, abdomen toward heart. All movement is toward the heart. Pressure of motion is just enough to lightly stimulate the skin and shouldn't be overly abrasive or leave a red mark.

NOTE: Do not use table salt. It is not the same as sea salt and will not be beneficial to your body. Also, rinse remaining salt in tub or shower down drain so it doesn't corrode the finish.

Related Healthy Habits:
- #22 Epsom Salt Soaks
- #24 Oilination

Resources:
- I like to experiment with various types of sea salt. You can use fine or medium grain salt. The rule of thumb is that the more natural color to the sea salt, the more nutrients it has. Look for non-iodized sea salt, not table salt.
- Many people prefer Pink Himalayan Sea Salt or Dead Sea Salt.

Creating a Cleaner
Greener Home

What:

Replace toxic chemicals for your home with non-toxic, uplifting substances that enhance your health instead of inhibit it. In home chemicals are constantly "outgassing" fumes in your home, garage and yard. If you are used to being around chemicals you may not even be able to noticeably smell them anymore. This is not a blessing.

Why?

Our children are being exposed to more chemicals in one day than our grandparents were exposed to in their entire lifetime. Here's the bigger issue: Even though each may have been approved individually, nobody has any idea how the combination of all of these chemicals in our environment is actually going to affect us over years of exposure. Visit Mercola.com or EWG.org to learn about the various ways chemical exposure can compromise your family's health.

How To:

- Learn to make your own household cleaning products from vinegar, baking soda and essential oils. See resources online or check out your local Natural Awakenings Magazines.

Simple Counter Top Cleaner:
Glass Spray bottle with 1 cup of white vinegar and 10 drops of essential oil (my favorite bacterial busters are lavender, peppermint, Purification Blend or lemon)

Mop Water Fresh:
Just add 1 tbs of white vinegar to mop bucket and 5 drops of your favorite essential oil. My favorites for mopping are lemongrass, geranium, lemon and peppermint.

All Purpose Cleaner and Great for Carpets
Thieves Household Cleaner is great diluted in a countertop spray bottle. We use it in mop water and even as our carpet cleaner. Also amazing to add to laundry or use along with vinegar on washer cleaning mode to rid the machine of mold and mildew odor and accumulation.

- You can purchase Green Cleaning products from companies like Dr. Bonners, Seven Generation, Ecover, Young Living.

Related Healthy Habits:
- #18 Personal Care Purification
- #84 Make Your Own Skincare Products

Resources:

- Environmental Working Group for scientific facts and realities of products you use and the hidden health challenges in them – ewg.org

- Cutting Edge Health News – Mercola.com
- Glass spray bottles available from – abundanthealth4u.com
- House Cleaning with Essential oils – 100EasyHealthyHabits. com
- Thieves Household Cleaner – abundanceandwisdom.com/ tararayburn
- How To Green Clean Your Home – treehugger.com/htgg/how-to-go-green-cleaning.html
- Distilled White Vinegar and baking soda
- Young Living – Therapeutic Grade Essential Oils , Quality personal care products and Diffusers – YoungLiving.com *Note: if you already work with a Young Living Distributor, please honor that relationship for ordering. If you are not currently working with a distributor or you are interested in becoming one, please see my website or see Resources in the back of the book.
- Essential Oil Desk Reference published by Life Science Publishing

Habit 18

Personal Care Product Purification

What:

Dr. Anne Stewart, of Loudoun Holistic Health in Va, teaches a class on toxins in our world. She expressed that the amount of toxins we absorb through our skin from our own personal care product is astronomical. Shampoo, body washes, rinses, etc., all carry many synthetic substances that can adversely fill our bodies' bucket rather than support it. Best places to become a quick study on the various effects of chemicals included in beauty and personal care products are Mercola.com and EWG.org

Why?

Our skin is our largest organ and used for detoxification. If you are putting toxins "on" your body, then they will be absorbed "in" your body. This will in turn accumulate and begin clogging your lymphatic system, stressing your body's filters and disrupting proper hormone function. When your hormones don't work right, you don't work right.

How To:

Visit the Environmental Working Group website to look up products and ingredients you use.

Best to purchase resource books or visit blogs to learn simple, money saving recipes for basic personal care supplies.

Related Healthy Habits:
- #17 Creating a Cleaner, Greener Home
- #84 Make Your Own Skin Care Products

Resources:

- Environmental Working Group for scientific facts and realities of products you use and the hidden health challenges in them – ewg.org
- **Beauty By God** by Shelly Ballestero
- **Earthly Bodies and Heavenly Hair** by Dina Falconi
- Cutting edge health information – Dr. Joseph Mercola's blog/ newsletters – Mercola.com
- The Healthy Habit Coach Blog – TheHealthyHabitCoach/ blog.com
- Young Living – Therapeutic Grade Essential Oils , Quality personal care products and Diffusers – YoungLiving.com Note: if you already work with a Young Living Distributor, please honor that relationship for ordering. If you are not currently working with a distributor or you are interested in becoming one, please see my website or see Resources in the back of the book.

Habit 19

Best Source Challenge

What:

The whole point of this book is to give you little habits to start with. When you begin to overhaul your way of eating, simply challenge yourself in one area at a time. Think about what you consume most and vow to educate yourself and get the best source of that item.

Why?

If you ingest something daily, it's going to have an effect on your health in some way. Invest in that one item improving your health rather than adding to chaos.

How To:

Ask yourself what you/your family consumes most/daily, then get the best source possible.

Use Dr. Pete Hilgartner's Good – Better – Best Principle.

Here's an example:

If your family consumes a lot of milk

Good: Buy Organic Milk

Better: Buy Organic Grass-Fed Milk with no rBGH growth hormone or antibiotics

Best: Farm Fresh Grass-Fed Milk from a local farm cow share. Make sure the cows are not being fed GMO feed.

Related Healthy Habits:
- #9 Eat REAL Food
- #13 Water Wisdom

Resources:

- Dr. Joseph Mercola's website/archives – mercola.com
- Weston A. Price Foundation – westonaprice.org
- Check out The Village Green Marketplace – villagegreennetwork. com
- Start following Village Green Network Bloggers like The Healthy Home Economist, Kelly the Kitchen Kop, Dr. Kaayla Daniel, Cheeseslave

Habit 20

Fasting

What:

A fast is a voluntary sacrifice for a set time period or is open ended as in a protest (Ghandi was famous for this). Although most of us think in terms of food or water when we hear about fasting, it really can be anything. Although they can have similar outcomes, the difference between fasting and cleansing, is usually the intent of spiritual enlightenment or clarity and physical and mental sacrifice.

Why?

People have used fasting as a way to sacrifice, gain clarity, regain health or spiritual focus for many, many years. Jesus fasted for 40 days in the desert. He was tempted and could have turned a rock into bread but stayed true to his fast and his faith in His Father. Catholics fast or "give up" something over Lent. Many people practice the Daniel 21 day fast of just fruits and vegetables. Most people feel like practicing fasts helps them with personal discipline and say that the physical benefits are gravy.

NOTE: A fast is not intended to be a permanent dietary practice. The intention isn't primarily health, and many fasts do not provide enough nutrients for long term life support. Even in the Bible the reason why Daniel didn't eat the "Royal" food and wine had more to do with a directive from God than his health.

How To:

Fasting is personal and preferential. The intentions for fasting are also very personal. There are liquid fasts, red meat fasts, electronic fasts, social media fasts, etc. The important thing to think about is what might you be worshiping or unwilling to give up? Perhaps that is the place to start.

I suggest reading the Book of Daniel in the Bible and the account of Jesus fasting for 40 days in the Bible Matthew 4-11.

Related Healthy Habits:
- #35 Grow and Practice Your Faith
- #43 The Cleanse

Resources:

- **The Daniel Fast** by Susan Gregory – daniel-fast.com
- **The Master Cleanse and Beyond the Master Cleanse** by Tom Woloshyn
- **The Bible** by God :-D

Habit 21

Exercise as a Habit

"Realize there is never a perfect time to implement an exercise program in today's busy life...but do it anyway."

– Dr. Pete Hilgartner, The Hilgartner Health Institute

What:

Exercise as a way of life is one of the most incredible practices you have to create a healthy foundation. By this, I do not mean extreme training or trying to exercise your way out of poor eating habits. What I mean is daily circulation and movement to help support the release of toxins, strengthen muscles and promote mental clarity. There are many ways to create circulation: cardio workouts, deep breathing, isometrics (using opposing muscle groups to strength train), dance, taking stairs instead of elevators, exercise classes of all kinds or simply nightly walks. My mom used to do mini muscle exercises during her daily chores like leg raises while doing the dishes, yoga facial exercises while driving...you get the idea.

Why?

Daily exercise can either be time specifically set aside, or interspersed throughout our daily activities. This practice is vital for a healthy, good quality of life. We are said to be God's Temple. How we treat that temple is a reflection of our respect for God. We get one body. How we honor God with it is quite important for all areas of health and well being.

How To:

I do not believe there is a "one size fits all" exercise or in the idea of "no pain – no gain." Perhaps that is because I'm slowly moving into my 50's. I believe it is because I have seen many extreme athletes or weekend warriors actually cause more harm to their health than good. I myself was one. What I do believe is that to realistically know oneself is the key to choosing and really incorporating exercise as a habit.

Here is a list of questions to think about when considering how to build exercise into your daily life:

- What type of job or typical day do you have? (Physical? On feet a lot? Sedentary? Around chemicals? Inside? Outside?)
- What is your typical stress level like?
- Are you better at solo or group exercise?
- Are you self disciplined or would you do better with a trainer?
- Do you have previous injuries or other physical challenges?
- Does your age affect what type of exercise might be best?

Great Healthy Exercise Resources:

- Dr. Pete Hilgartner – The Hilgartner Health Institute – HilgartnerHealth.com

- Pilates Master Aliesa George – Centerworks Functional Fitness – centerworks.com
- The Nia Technique – nianow.com
- Your local YMCA or Community Center

NOTES:

Habit 22

Epsom Salt Soaks

What:

Epsom Salt is one of the top ten choices in my family home health cabinet. I remember it as one of those old fashioned remedies my Granny Pearl passed to my mom, who passed to me. We add it along with some warm water to a big bowl or pot and soak our sprains, pains and bruised bodies. It relaxes and reduces pain and inflammation. Added to a bath, it can help a "full bucket" detox and relax.

Why?

My family has created such a strong anchored physiological response to the Epsom Salt bath, just the idea of having one brings stress reduction and smiles. Stress is a huge factor in our health whether it is physical, emotional or spiritual. Soaking is a gentle way to calm, soothe and detox the body, mind and soul. You can add a side of herbal tea to sip on, relaxing music and candles and create your own spa experience. Water jets can assist the lymphatic system in more detox.

How To:

For General Use: Add 1 lb of Epsom Salt and 1-2 drops of mild essential oil (like lavender or Sacred Mountain Blend) to salt and then add to tub. Since oil and water don't mix, adding oil to salt gives it a nice vehicle to disperse into tub.

For More Detox: Add 1 lb of Epsom Salt, 1 lb of Baking Soda, 1-2 tbs of Sea Salt and 1-2 drops of mild essential oil
- Good to steep in it for an uninterrupted 20 minutes and sweat a little.
- I like to add a sea salt scrub just before getting out.
- Rinse toxic release in shower.
- Dry off and do an Oilination to cap off the pampering.

Related Healthy Habits:
- #16 Salt Scrubbing
- #24 Oilination

Resources:
- Epsom Salt is available at most stores in the Pharmacy or First Aid sections
- Sea Salt – Can use fine or medium grain salt. The rule of thumb is that the more natural color to the sea salt, the more nutrients it has. Look for non-iodized sea salt, not table salt.
- Young Living – Therapeutic Grade Essential Oils , Quality personal care products and Diffusers – YoungLiving.com *Note: if you already work with a Young Living Distributor, please honor that relationship for ordering. If you are not currently working with a distributor or you are interested in becoming one, please see my website or see Resources in the back of the book.

Habit 23

Chew, Chew, Chew

In fond memory of
Health Pioneer Dr. Bruce MacFarland

What:

Dr. Bruce MacFarland was a nutritionist most of his life. I asked him once, in all his years, what did he feel was the #1 best advice he could give someone regarding their health. He smiled and slowly repeated "Chew…Chew…Chew!" At first I thought… Really? Now I know that was one of the most brilliant answers I've ever heard. Properly and mindfully chewing your food can support weight loss, reduce stress, improve healthy hair, skin and nails by not overworking your liver. Brilliant!

Why?

The fact is, no matter what kind of diet you are eating, if you are not being mindful in chewing it well (some say to a liquid state!), you are likely not digesting and absorbing the nutrients very well. Keep in mind, many foods have very little to no digestive enzymes and on top of that, most people have hectic lifestyles and are eating on the go – not great for our health. So then, we spend money on enzymes or antacids. Hmmm, much cheaper and quicker to simply chew…chew…chew.

I'm a mom and feel like mealtime can be gulping and giving out corrections or answering questions with my mouth full half the time. I know, practice what I preach, right? Also, I'm married to the world's greatest "chewer." Our friend, Dr. Dave Stewart in Virginia, once told us that Mike absorbed nutrients just about better than anyone he'd ever seen before. We believe it has to do with how well he chews. Granted, it takes a lot longer eating a meal alongside Mike, but the health benefits are worth it. It also causes me to be better with my chewing.

How To:
Chew……Chew……Chew……

Related Healthy Habits:
- #2 Manage Your Bucket
- #8 Digestion Suggestions

Resources:
- Your Mouth for Mindful and Active chewing of your meals ;-)

Habit 24

Oilination

What:

Oilination is a term I learned from the Dhyana Center's website referring to applying a massage and essential oil mixture over the body to support circulation, detoxification and overall health.

Why?

Supporting your lymphatic system is a HUGE part of your health and wellness. In short, this is the system which circulates and helps eliminate toxins from the body. As you can guess from this series, in today's world we tend to accumulate more toxins than we are aware of, and need to find more creative ways to rid our body of these offenders.

How To:

1. I use a small glass canning jar to pour about a 1/4 cup of massage oil. I love kukui in the warmer months and castor oil in the colder months for extra moisture. I then add 5-10 drops total of my favorite essential oils. This can be tailored to your preference. My favorite combinations are: lemongrass and basil, Release Blend and lavender, or eucalyptus and lemon. Be creative. If you have sensitive skin test on small area first

and start with less essential oil in the mixture.

2. Next, after the shower and drying off or first thing in the morning, I'll start massaging in the mixture from feet to torso, hands toward heart, chest toward abdomen, abdomen toward heart. All movement is toward the heart.

3. Allow oils to penetrate the skin before putting on clothes or you might have some permanent oil stains on your clothes.

Related Healthy Habits:
*   #16 Salt Scrubbing
*   #22 Epsom Salt Soaks

Resources:
*   Castor Oil from The Heritage Store – heritagestore.com or BAAR – baar.com
*   Kukii Oil from Oils of Aloha – oilsofaloha.com
*   Young Living – Therapeutic Grade Essential Oils , Quality personal care products and Diffusers – YoungLiving.com *Note: if you already work with a Young Living Distributor, please honor that relationship for ordering. If you are not currently working with a distributor or you are interested in becoming one, please see my website or see Resources in the back of the book.
*   Oilination video from Dhyana Center – dhyanacenter.com or or Google Olination Video
*   Also check out Dry Brushing before showering or bathing

Habit 25

Make Your Own Veggie Wash

What:

We all are beginning to realize how the toxins in our environment can settle on our foods whether or not they have been grown organically. These toxins range from heavy metals, to chemicals, to animal droppings and unbeneficial organisms. They can be sprayed during growth or absorbed via atmospheric conditions.

Why?

These substances can affect your health by filling your body with hormone disruptors and heavy metals that are not easily detoxed. In one day, children are exposed to more chemicals than our grandparents encountered in their whole life. The truth is that no one has any clue what the consequences will be of the combinations of chemicals and the long term exposures. Why not do your best to remove what is easy with only a topical substance? We can reduce this burden easily by simply washing our food before we ingest it.

How to:

To clean and refresh your fruits and vegetables, you can make your own produce wash easily with vinegar and essential oils. Fill sink or large glass container with cleanest source of water you can. Avoid tap water as it usually has chlorine and flouride. Add 1 tablespoon of white vinegar and 5-8 drops of therapeutic grade lemon essential oil. Other citrus oils can be used or mixed in too.

> **TIP:** Learn about Genetically Modified Foods (GMO's) – nonGMOProject.com

Resources:

- Young Living – Therapeutic Grade Essential Oils , Quality personal care products and Diffusers – YoungLiving.com *Note: if you already work with a Young Living Distributor, please honor that relationship for ordering. If you are not currently working with a distributor or you are interested in becoming one, please see my website or see Resources in the back of the book.
- 1001 Uses for White Distilled Vinegar – vinegartips.com
- **Organic White Vinegar** by Spectrum – vitacost.com

Creating Your Healthy Habits Worksheet

You can use this a a template to copy for your health journal or download clean copies from 100EasyHealthyHabits.com

Make a prioritized list of 3-6 personal health goals and or challenges.

1. _____

2. _____

3. _____

4. _____

5. _____

6. _____

Next, choose one habit to focus on for one week.

Now brainstorm 5-10 Healthy Habits that would support this goal/ challenge (Use shorthand by listing them using as Habits in the book – HH #72 page 191)

1. _____

2. _____

3. _____

4. _____

5. _____

6. _____

7. _____

8. _____

9. _____

10. _____

Action Step: Just Do It! Pick one habit and practice it for one week.

After one week Evaluate:
Did the habit work for you? Do you want to keep it or lose it? What worked? What didn't work and why?

Now pick another habit from your list of supporting habits and repeat.

100 Easy Healthy Habits book and Audio Coaching Series are your roadmap to a better quality of life. You can choose one habit a week, one a month even one a year. The main goal is to add healthy habits and to anchor positive associations with creating a healthier mind, body and soul. As you get more comfortable with the process you may want to challenge yourself to shoot for adding monthly habits. Be sure to set yourself up for success and choose your habits wisely. Don't bite off more than you can chew or set wimpy goals.

Enjoy sharing your changes with others as you become a Ripple of Health in our World!

"A peaceful heart leads to a healthy body"

– Proverbs 14:30

Healthy Habits for Peace of Mind

Introduction

The habits contained in this section may not always seem directly related to your health at first. When you start practicing them you will experience how intricately connected our emotional, spiritual and mental health is to our physical well being. Many people compartmentalize their health and I'd like to encourage you to focus on the big picture, rather than micromanaging symptoms.

Two of the most powerful concepts in Healthy Habits for Peace of Mind is #32 The Power of Anchors and … all the rest :-D Seriously, it is a good section. Learning about anchoring, also called Neurolinguistic Programming (NLP), is vital to creating better health through positive associations with new habits. Please digest this concept well.

Another key point to remember is to release your stress. Stressing about the process will not help, but will hinder the process. The physical manifestations of feeling stressed can counteract the healthy habits you are adding. Healthy Habits are meant to be explored, played with and gained from. Stress-Less Living is of greater impact to your health than any sit up or green smoothie. Open your mind and heart to creating REAL Health with love and laughter along the way.

Habit 26

Teach Don't Preach

What:

Share your experience and knowledge with your family, friends and spheres of influence with humor and humility. Make the message fun and welcomed, rather than shooting lessons out through fear and my-way-or-the-highway mentality.

Why:

It's hard not to come across like a steamroller when you have learned lessons through blood, sweat and tears. Unwanted messages are a waste of everyone's time, talent and energy. I used to come home from Wise Tradition, Young Living and other health conventions ready to change the world, which is a nice thought, except that not everyone else was receptive to the message. Choose your lessons and your battles wisely. Be patient. Walk the talk and wait for the signs of an open, receptive listener.

How To:

- Always ask permission to share your advice/opinion.
- When sharing with your family, start with one Habit at a time instead of a complete makeover.
- If health reasons or circumstances dictate you add healthy

changes faster, then try and be humble, fun and rather matter of fact about the new ways of doing things. No guilt allowed.

- Smile and remember: "Laughter really is the best medicine."
- Recognize that glazed over look when someone has heard too much at one time. Stop and reframe one simple change a person can make.
- Recognize the "I have no desire to hear what you have to say" look and don't waste your time and energy on the conversation.
- Walk your talk and stay the course. Many people will ask you when they end up experiencing health issues or challenges or see that you are not simply preaching the next new fad.
- Admit when and where you aren't walking your talk and share your challenges. This actually helps people relate better and even trust your message more.
- Pray for discernment. Ask God to help you know when, where and how to share the message of health with others.

Related Healthy Habits:
- #1 Simply Start
- #6 Dial in Nutrient Rich Foods
- #9 Eat REAL Food

Resources:
- 100 Easy Healthy Habits: Uplifting Habits for the Mind, Body and Soul – Audio coaching series and book by Tara Rayburn – 100EasyHealthyHabits.com
- The Healthy Habit Coach Blog – thehealthyhabitcoach.com/blog
- **The Complete Master Cleanse** by Tom Woloshyn – themastercleanse.org

- Environmental Working Group – ewg.org
- Dr. Pete and Lolin Hilgartner and The Hilgartner Health Institute – hilgartnerhealth.com
- **Healthy Healing** by Linda Page, Ph.D

NOTES:

Habit 27

Waking Well

What:

Start your day with gratitude, grounding and uplifting habits. This can enhance how you respond to the people, circumstances, challenges and joys of the day. Resist the temptation to turn on the news or to start going over your calendar and "to do lists" when you first wake. I wake just a 1/2 hour early so I have time for what I call my "God & Goals Time" which consists of morning devotion, Bible reading, handwriting my top 10 goals and reading my Strategic Attraction Plan. (For SAP see Stacey Hall and Chi-To-Be.)

Why:

How we wake up and what we do those first moments of the day sets a tone that can be uplifting or cause us to feel like the rug has been pulled out from under us. When we allow ourselves to wake well, we set a foundation of grounding and joy that is difficult to change regardless of the day's or night's events. When I miss my "God & Goal Time," I really notice a difference, and unfortunately my family might too. You may tailor the habit's content and time to suit your lifestyle, but having it be the first thing you do or focus on is pretty important, otherwise life has a tendency to "happen" around you and perhaps sidetrack you into other activities that are far less grounding.

My Morning Ritual:

- Set a harp alarm about 1/2 hour before I have to get started on my morning activities. This is before the rest of the household.
- Apply the essential oil of my choice over my forehead, back of neck and over my heart.
- Sit where I can view the sunrise and hear the morning birds and critters.
- Have a cup of organic coffee, tea or cultured beverage.
- Read my daily devotional.
- Read the day's entry for my Bible reading plan.
- Handwrite my top ten goals.
- Read my whole SAP (Strategic Attraction Plan).

NOTE: I've found a way to dial in almost all of my senses to anchor the experience on all levels. That way, if I'm feeling stressed later, I can use one of these anchors and immediately have a sense of calm and grounding. It's like "mental muscle memory," doing something so often that your body simply can go into auto pilot.

How To:

- I like to anchor as many senses into this habit such as sights, sounds, smells, tastes and feeling. (See my example above.)
- If you have an alarm, switch to music or set it to a pleasant sound to awaken you.
- If you are using your phone or computer as an alarm, put it across the room not beside you.

- Don't sleep with the alarm clock right in your sight. Every time you wake and look at it your mind starts to dial in a million thoughts.
- If you can, let the morning sunlight wake you up by leaving curtains open slightly.
- No matter how much sleep you are going to be able to get, let the last thought before you go to sleep be a self suggestion that you will have all the sleep you need to feel rested.
- Allow the first thought of the day to be of "Gratitude" for the day, for your life and all its blessings and challenges.
- Build in some gentle movement and deep breathing exercises to get the oxygen flowing.
- If you go over your schedule the night before and write down any notes/reminders/etc., you can forgo jumping out of bed in an "oh my gosh" state of mind. Stacey Hall shares how to plan for success in the Chi-To-Be books and audio coaching series. She also shares other great energy surges.

Related Healthy Habits:
- #14 Life Breathing = Breathing Life
- #21 Exercise as a Habit
- #32 The Power of Anchors

Resources:
- **The Bible** by God
- **Jesus Calling** by Sarah Young is a great devotional.
- Chi-To-Be: Attracting the Perfect B-All book, workbook and audio coaching by Stacey Hall
- **Attracting the Perfect Customers** by Stacey Hall and Jan Brogniez
- Brian Tracy for goal setting and success – briantracy.com

Habit 28

Get Un-Plugged!

Plan for an electronics or social media fast and see how much you really might be depending on being "plugged in."

What:

We have the world at our fingertips and have many messages vying for our attention all day, everyday. I grew up with just advertisements in between TV shows. Kids today are growing up with multiple streams of communication constantly begging for attention: ads or news scrolling across the bottom of the screen, texts, incoming e-mail and notifications, music, electronic books, videos, games, apps and ads on everything you can see including buildings. We live in Las Vegas, and there are lights, cameras and action going on 24 hours a day.

Media of every kind is used for the good, and perhaps, for the not so good. Adults oftentimes use it to escape, or worse, not be present with the real people they are with. Kids are so plugged in that media of all kinds have become their makeshift nanny. The constant input, especially of aggressive subjects actually alters the brain waves and can affect behavior. This barrage of constant input can lead to aggressive or passive behavior, and even feelings of despair or depression.

Why:

Years ago, I read The Artist's Way by Julia Cameron, and one of the exercises was to take a week long media fast. This book was about how to unblock your creativity and explained that, if you are constantly on input mode, this could be short circuiting your output mode. I, who used to watch the news everyday multiple times and had favorite shows each night, felt a panic at the idea of this. That is why I knew I needed to do it. And yes, it helped un-block my creativity.

Years later a friend at a conference shared with me that he used "screen time" as a disciplinary action for his kids. "You forgot to clean your room again? No screen time for a day." Sounds silly, but those of you with kids know the kind of leverage the words "your phone will be mine" or "no electronics" can hold. Taking this step into a more positive lesson, be mindful of how much time your kids spend in front of screens of any kind, shape or size. Make sure they are present with friends more than next to them, each playing their own game. Have them spend time appreciating a real book, playing an instrument or creating something real.

How To:

Un-Plug for a day, a week, a month…sound scary? Then maybe this is a really good habit to practice.

Related Healthy Habits:
- #20 Fasting
- #43 The Cleanse

Resources:

- **The Artist's Way** by Julia Cameron
- No more input for the time period you fast. Just be un-plugged.

NOTES:

Habit 29

Release, Rest and Rejuvenate

**The Three R's of Sustainable Healthy Living...
Release, Rest and Rejuvenate.**

What:

When you truly **Release** the stressors in you life, you can then really **Rest** so that you have the energy for **Rejuvenation** and can live a very fulfilling and sustainable life.

Release: This is the intentional ability and activity of letting go of what is no longer necessary or irrelevant or an outright energy drag on your mind, body and soul. This is not shirking responsibility by putting your head in the sand but rather a very important habit of cleansing your mind, body and soul of the "tolls and toxins" that you have been accumulating throughout your day. I have created a "Release Ritual" designed for you to let go of whatever stress, complication, baggage may have attached itself to you via the event, interaction or endeavor. (see **How to** section)

Rest: This is a complete and effective unplugging from the world, our roles, thoughts, tasks and To Do's. This is not a shirking of responsibilities either but a temporary rest from carrying them around. I am a big believer in the **Power Nap** where I shut off my brain for about 15 minutes: 5 minutes to unravel, 5 to go deep and 5 to come out of it. Most of us are multitasking from the minute we open our eyes until the moment we lay our head on the pillow. Unplugging can not only energize us, but give us clarity, focus and support our endocrine system. It is very important to **Release** before **Rest** so that you can truly unplug.

Rejuvenation: This is the practice of restoring youthful vigor; Or making fresh or new again. The way one rejuvenates can vary. Some people prefer some alone time curled up with a book, while other recharge being with people for activity or events. You get to choose what rejuvenates you! ;-)

Why:

Years ago I heard a speaker from Urban Zen at the Young Living Grand Convention who made the point, "As a culture, we have confused rest with collapse." I couldn't agree more. This spoke to me in a huge way. I would go, go, go and finally get a moment to sit and absolutely collapse. This puts you into "On – Off" mode... period. Go or Stop with no in between isn't a very sustainable way to live.

If you aren't **Releasing** the day's events or stress, then it is very difficult to **Rest** let alone **Rejuvenate**. Without **Rest** and **Rejuvenation** we can live in a state of exhaustion on every level and become a human "doing" instead of a human "being."

How To:

Release Ritual: A symbolic activity you create by engaging as many of the senses as possible and then by visualizing the release of physical, emotional, mental and spiritual associations that no longer serve you, are destructive or just plain do not need to linger in your life or consciousness.

For example, when I have been involved in a very emotional volunteer experience as I oftentimes am with The Cupcake Girls in Las Vegas, I drive home down Las Vegas Blvd and imagine whatever cares, worries, stresses or unnecessary stuff hanging on to me is sloughed off and blows away with the wind. I actually visualize thoughts falling away as I drive. By the time I get home I am ready for rest.

Invest in Rest and Rest Proactively:
Three important steps for Rest:
1. Find a place peaceful to you. For someone like my husband, he loves to rest on a couch in the middle of mayhem, kids and conversation. For me, it's a Power Nap in my bed or a comfortable spot outside where feet go up and eyelids go down.

2. Set a timer. If you have a certain amount of time, need to be somewhere, or just want to train yourself to be able to reboot in 15, then set a timer with a pleasant alarm to wake you up. Allow for a couple minutes to get your wits about you without having to jump up and run.

3. Self suggest that whatever amount of time you have, 5, 10,

15, 30 minutes or an hour, will be exactly what you need to reboot, reset and rest your system.

Investing in rest is priceless and rewards not only us but those around us. As far as other people go, it also means sometimes saying "No" to invitations at the risk of them not understanding or feeling hurt. Be kind and confident as you model health in this way.

Rejuvenation:

Although rejuvenation can be achieved through much needed sleep, it is really solidified by being rested and having the energy and vitality to engage in an activity that absolutely feeds your soul. For me a trip to the beach with salt air, warm sand and water is awesome. In Vegas, where we don't have a beach I find going to a "good" show is a great way to rejuvenate or even just taking an **Epsom Salt Soak.** For others they seek adventures like whitewater rafting, mountaineering or a mission trip to a developing country. Brian Tracy prescribes a vacation of no less than two weeks at a time once or twice a year.

TIPS & TRICKS:
- Do you consider these three R's luxuries or well invested time? I can tell you the healthiest people I know practice these three habits.
- Anchoring is one of my favorite tools to support all three of these habits. Anchoring is the practice of engaging as many of the senses as possible while practicing a habit such as grounding, release, rest, rejuvenation, etc. Then you can call up an aroma, visual cue, or song to help you feel that sense of Release, Rest and Rejuvenation even when you are in the middle of a storm.

I like using essential oils for this because I can bring them whereever I go. Some of the Young Living Essential Oil names even lend themselves to these practices. Like Release, Sacred Mountain, Dreamweaver and Believe. ;-)

My Top Five Essential Oil Blend Picks are:
- **Release:** Ylang Ylang, Lavindin, Geranium, Sandalwood, Blue Tansy in Olive Oil base
- **Believe:** Ingredients: Idaho Balsam Fir, Rosewood and Frankincense
- **Valor:** Spruce, Rosewood, Blue Tansy and Frankincense in Almond Oil base
- **Peace and Calming:** Tangerine, Orange, Ylang Ylang, Patchouli, and Blue Tansy
- **Sacred Mountain:** Spruce, Ylang Ylang, Balsam Fir and Cedarwood

Related Healthy Habits:
- #22 Epsom Salt Soak
- #32 The Power of Anchors

Resources:
- Release, Rest & Rejuvenate post on my blog – thehealthyhabitcoach.com/health-and-wellness/release-rest-rejuvenation
- Young Living – Therapeutic Grade Essential Oils , Quality personal care products and Diffusers – YoungLiving.com *Note: if you already work with a Young Living Distributor, please honor that relationship for ordering. If you are not currently working with a distributor or you are interested in becoming one, please see my website or see Resources in

the back of the book.

- Urban Zen – urbanzen.org
- Brian Tracy for goal setting and success – briantracy.com
- Mike Rayburn CD's for all 3 R's – MikeRayburn.com

NOTES:

Habit 30

Engage the Whole Family

What:

Raising the bar and creating healthy habits in the household cannot be one person's task. This transformation works best when the whole household is empowered and engaged. I know we have a rule in my home, "If you didn't help shop, chop, prepare or cook… no complaints allowed."

Why:

There are a few reasons to engage the whole family. It's taken me several years to really understand these points. Hopefully, it will help your learning curve.

1. Taking part in the process creates ownership in each member. They helped create it which usually makes them far less critical. Practice for everyone creates a strong habit.

2. If you are the one mandating all the changes and orchestrating the new habits, you can become more like a dictator than a family member. Nobody likes living under a dictator.

3. Learning and implementing new recipes and habits can

be exhausting on all levels when you go it alone. I recently re-learned this lesson. I had tendonitis (don't ask ;-0) and could not chop, lift, or pour out my stock pots. Even washing dishes hurt. How humbling and what an eye-opening experience to see how much I was doing and not sharing the tasks with my family. How are my kids going to learn how to cook if I'm not engaging them more often? Strive to teach not preach and create life long health habits for the whole household.

How To:

- Ask, assign tasks and create an attitude in the air for voluntary assistance.
- Reward outstanding help and initiatives by family members or roommates.
- Take a cooking or exercise class together.
- Laugh and create a fun atmosphere.
- Create family/household exercise time like walks, family dance night, foot massage trade offs.
- Come up with a fun phrase to acknowledge that someone isn't happy. We love a line from the movie **Despicable Me** where Gruel just says "Don't Care!" in his thick accent. Our family knows that when that is said, it's done in a light-hearted way and is meant to cut the tension instantly.
- Encourage each household member to come up with the "Habit of the Month" and take turns focusing on each member's habit or recipe.

Related Healthy Habits:
- # 1-100 ;-)

Resources:

- The Healthy Habit Coach Blog – thehealthyhabitcoach.com/blog
- Village Green Network Bloggers have great tips & tricks – villagegreennetwork.com
- Monday Mania on Pinterest – I share this board with The Healthy Home Economist and other great idea creators – pinterest.com/HealthyHomeEcon/monday-mania

---

NOTES:

Habit 31

Eat, Sleep, Drink -
Ms. Mary's Mantra

What:

Mary Vars, my friend and co-author of **Essential Gluten-Free Recipes** practices and shares her mantra for healthy foundations: Eat REAL food, get plenty of sleep and hydrate well by drinking plenty of water. We lovingly call this "Ms. Mary's Mantra" and it is the cornerstone of uplifting and sustainable healthy habits.

Why:

Many people have coached with me over the years and sought supplements, essential oils or some diet or exercise they can follow for relief of their symptoms. I have learned to start by looking at the larger picture and I ask the following questions:

- How is your diet? How well are you eating? What are you eating?
- Are you getting enough sleep? Are you getting rest? How is your stress level?
- Do you drink water? How much? What else do you drink daily?

The answers to these questions almost always give us our places to start adjusting habits.

How To:

Know Yourself. This is not some fluffy phrase, but a reality. Know how much sleep your body really wants. Know what types of foods uplift you and support you "doing life" instead of being exhausted all the time. Make your beverages count! We included a whole section in our book **Essential Gluten-Free Recipes** called Bountiful Beverages because we know the value of hydrating and nourishing through the liquids we consume or not consume daily.

Related Healthy Habits:
- #3 Nutritional Anchors
- #6 Dial in Nutrient Rich Foods
- #13 Water Wisdom
- #25 Release, Rest and Rejuvenate

Resources:
- Mary Vars, Mentor Mom – mkvars@verizon.net
- Chef Shane Kelly – chefshanekelly.com
- The Healthy Habit Coach – thehealthyhabitcoach.com
- The mirror and your journal

Habit 32

The Power of Anchors

What:

Anchoring is when you create or link strong associations with events, activities or substances. The fact is that you create anchors all the time without even being aware of it. I like to use as many senses as possible to anchor in a positive association with a habit or result from a habit. If your beloved grandmother used to make chicken soup and you have a good association with that, then you have a positive anchor. However, if you did not have a very good relationship with granny, then you may have a pretty negative anchor/association with the smell or taste of chicken soup. A closely related form of this is called Neuro-Linguistic Programming (NLP).

Why:

Again, we create anchors subconsciously all of the time. Unfortunately, all of them are not always beneficial anchors. For example, what do you associate with exercise? You can anchor an association of pain, weight loss, feeling strong, a better quality of life or just about anything really. Once conscious of this, and aware of your existing anchors, the choice of what and how you anchor is YOURS! Fabulous point here, once you realize what you have anchored to a particular habit, you can choose to change it, tweak it, or create a totally new anchor in its place.

How To:

I like to associate as many senses with this process as possible. That way I have more than just one particular element I can use to trigger a particular feeling or desired action. It's like Pavlov's dog, but with more triggers than just a bell ;-) I can also amplify the effects of a particularly healthy habit by creating multiple anchors for one desired outcome.

Example:

Desired Habit: I want to start my day feeling grounded and peaceful so I am going to get up early and practice my faith, write out my goals and read my Strategic Attraction Plan (SAP).

Logistics: I will wake up a half hour before everyone else and before I need to start getting ready for the day.

Goal: To anchor a positive association with getting up early and investing that time towards peace of mind and to have tangible tools to recreate this sense of grounding and peace throughout my day.

Supplies: Calm method for waking, my morning devotional, Bible, SAP on my iPad, journal, a good pen, cup of tea or coffee, favorite robe, comfortable chair and favorite view or spot in the house.

Process: I wake to a harp sounding alarm, give God gratitude for my life and a new day, put on my favorite robe which represents reward for hard work to me, make coffee or herbal tea and choose an essential oil for the morning. I put a few drops in my left palm to inhale and then apply over my heart, shoulders and back of head and neck. I sit where I can see the sun rising over the mountain and hear the morning sounds of birds, coyotes or silence. I read my devotional and Bible and write down significant thoughts or quotes in my journal. I handwrite my top ten goals with "God Willing" written at the top and "To His Glory" at the bottom followed by my signature.

NOTE: I believe that God can give us this sense of well being without any extra tools, anchors or elements, but we humans do well with anchoring the intangible with something tangible.

Here's a look at the elements I can use to instantly recreate grounding and wellbeing throughout my day.

- Sound: pleasant alarm
- Touch: favorite clothing with positive anchor and comfortable couch or chair. A good pen to write with – doesn't have to be expensive, just feel good and write well.
- Smell: essential oil and herbal tea and morning air
- Taste: pleasing hot or cold beverage
- Sight: uplifting view and morning birds, bugs and bees

After a while this process becomes like a muscle memory and even if I don't have all the elements, I still can feel that sense of well being.

Related Healthy Habits:

- #27 Waking Well
- #35 Grown and Practice Your Faith
- #90 Attitude of Gratitude

Resources:

- **The Bible** by God ;-)
- **Jesus Calling** or other morning devotionals by Sarah Young
- Neuro-linguistic Programming (NLP) concept created by Richard Bandler
- **Chi-To-Be** book, audio series and coaching By Stacey Hall – chi-to-be.com
- **Slique Tea** by Young Living

Habit 33

Create Healthy Rewards

What:

Create and anchor uplifting rewards for accomplishments or hard days: massage, naps, baths, listen to favorite music, healthy treats and quality time with loved ones. Many people have anchored very unhealthy habits like overspending, addictions or health compromising foods and beverages as a "reward" for just about anything. "I had a hard day so I'm going to have a _____" or "I've earned the right to do _____" or my child feels sad so I'll make him a bowl of _____."

So I ask you, how do you fill in those blanks?

Why:

How you fill in those blanks for yourself and your family can set you up for a life of health or a life of symptoms and possibly addictions. Early on in life I anchored ice cream as a big reward. A reward I allowed myself and justified for just about anything. Not an unusual reward in our culture except for someone like me who actually had reactions from consuming pasteurized dairy. Later my reward became wine. Again, very acceptable in our world, except for someone who finds a way to reward themselves with it more often than not. Get the idea?

How To:

- Make a list of uplifting rewards for yourself and household members.
- Post them so everyone can see until they become habitual.
- Find a gentle way to remind each other that instead of (Blank) as a special gift or reward you'd prefer (Blank), i.e., instead of chocolate cake, you'd really rather have flowers.
- Keep practicing and creating positive anchors with your new rewards and habits.
- You can also do the reverse, create negative anchors/ associations with the old habits. For Example: "I REALLY hate the headache or how I feel after having wine or too much sugar."
- Try to come up with non food/beverage rewards too.
- Practice, Practice, Practice

Related Healthy Habits:
- #32 The Power of Anchors
- #46 Create Healthy Traditions

Resources:

- The Healthy Habit Coach Blog – thehealthyhabitcoach.com/blog
- KC Healthy Kids – kchealthykids.org
- Chef Shane Kelly – chefshanekelly.com
- Healthy Holiday Treats and Gifts – pinterest.com/tararayburn/holiday-treats-and-gifts

Get Curious -
Listen to 3's

What:

So what's next? What is pertinent for you and your health? Listen, look and be aware of themes that keep presenting themselves to you. I used to tell people what habits I thought they should do or perhaps "should" release. After a conversation with my friend and amazing speech and presentation coach, Patricia Fripp, I had a major thought shift. The best habit for anyone to start with or add is…the habit they will actually practice. No matter what I tell them, if the habit isn't relevant to them, chances are they won't do it.

Why:

So why do I think that concept was such a pivotal point in my coaching approach? It was pivotal because I believe each person is truly an individual and has the access to a divine connection with their Maker. When a lesson or habit needs to be added or released, it seems as though it will keep presenting itself…over and over and over and over…until you finally get the message and take action. It took me almost 40 years to really get that concept, and now I've learned to look for 3's. If a personally significant topic appears at least three times within a short amount of time, I not only become curious, but I know it's time to pay good attention to this topic and its relevance for my life.

How To:

- Pray for and set your intention for clarity to see what themes are important for you to pay attention to. These can range from what seems to be small like your choice of a water bottle to something huge like avoiding genetically modified foods (GMO's) and experiencing relief from chronic symptoms that you were previously unable to get a handle on.
- Visualize yourself as a fine-tuned device able to cut through the "noise" of the world and hear the messages intended for your wellbeing.
- Keep a daily journal for rolling these thoughts around or skimming occasionally to see what themes have been presenting themselves that you might have missed.

Related Healthy Habits:
- #1-100 :-D

Resources:

- Dr. Joseph Mercola's Website – mercola.com
- Verve Messages Online – vimeo.com/channels/watchverve
- Non-GMO Project – nongmoproject.org
- Dr. Kaayla Daniel – drkaayladaniel.com
- Weston A. Price Foundation – westonaprice.org
- The OGG Blog – ofgodsgrace.blogspot.com

Habit 35

Grow and Practice Your Faith

"If you but love God, you may do as you incline."

– St. Augustine

What:

To want to change core behavior for the better requires relationship with God. To have a relationship requires time spent together. We can build communication and relationship with Him by engaging in daily habits that strengthen our faith. We align ourselves with great strength and perseverance when we ground ourselves in God. We can build communication and relationship with Him by engaging in daily habits that strengthen our faith.

Why:

It took me a few years to realize that I could not coach anyone on health and wellness and leave God out. The clients who have some level of faith have always been successful with more velocity and ease than those without faith. No matter what it is, I can always do it better and more sustainably with God.

How To:

- Decide to find a relationship with God regardless of where you are right this moment.
- Start a daily habit with the intention of being open to Him. (read, write, walk, pray)
- Find someone you admire and ask them what faith habits they practice. Notice I said faith habits, rather than following their faith.
- Accept the grace of knowing that "God loves you just the way you are. He just loves you too much to leave you that way." – Vince Antonucci
- Be consistent. Shoot for 80:20. Practice the habits at least 80% of the time. Strive for it being an unusual occurrence that you don't practice habits of your faith.
- Start by loving people unconditionally. "And now these three remain: faith, hope and love. And the greatest of these is LOVE."- 1 Corinthians 13: 13

Related Healthy Habits:
- #27 Waking Well
- #36 Grace

Resources:

- **The Bible** by God
- **The Road Less Traveled** by M. Scott Peck
- Renegade Guerilla Lovers by Vince Antonucci
- **The Ragamuffin Gospel** and **The Furious Longing of God** by Brennan Manning
- **Embracing the Grey: A Wing, A Prayer and a Doubters Resolve** by Mark Hollingsworth
- The OGG Blog – ofgodsgrace.blogspot.com

Habit 36

Grace

"Grace finds goodness in everything... Grace makes beauty out of ugly things."

– Grace, **Bono, U2**

What:

"Even though you are supposed to pay, not having to pay." – from Philip Yancey's blog. This meaning of grace is complex, yet simple. Grace is a gift that cannot be earned. Grace is a gift of love and acceptance without strings. Accepting this unconditional love without any expectations in return is an act of faith. After receiving this gift, we never want to be the same. "God loves you just the way you are. He just loves you too much to leave you that way." – Vince Antonucci

Once we are able to receive grace, we are finally able to extend it to others.

Why:

"Christ accepts us as we are, but when he accepts us, we cannot remain as we are." – Walter Trobisch.

The ability to receive and give grace is intricately connected to our health and quality of life.

How To:

- To extend grace to others, we must first truly receive it from God.
- "To love a person means to see him as God intended him to be." – Dostoevsky
- Become a student of grace. I read this goal in my SAP daily.

Related Healthy Habits:
- #35 Grow and Practice Your Faith

Resources:

- **The Bible** by God
- Grace by U2 Videos – ofgodsgrace.blogspot.com/2013/04/grace-makes-beauty-from-ugly-things.html
- The OGG Blog (of God's Grace) – ofgodsgrace.blogspot.com
- **What's So Amazing About Grace?** by Phillip Yancey
- Philip Yancey's blog – philipyancey.com/q-and-a-topics/grace
- **The Furious Longing for God** by Brennan Manning

Habit 37

Have Healthy Boundaries

What:

Knowing when to say yes or no, stop or go, enough or more and making that clear to those around you in a mature and effective way. Sound simple? Today we can see the extremes of this idea of boundaries on the nightly news as stories are told of victims and perpetrators. Both victims and perpetrators are examples of having unhealthy boundaries. Victims – unable to define, request or sometimes enforce healthy boundaries. Perpetrators – unable to respect or honor other people's healthy boundaries…usually a result of having unhealthy boundary issues themselves.

The challenge in creating healthy boundaries and living with other people is how effectively and respectfully you can share and honor each other's boundaries. My-way-or-the-highway mentality usually backfires, if not at first, it does ultimately.

Why:

"By recognizing the need to set and enforce limits, you protect your self-esteem, maintain self-respect, and enjoy healthy relationships." – Terri Cole.

How To:

Learning where you start and someone else begins is not a given. Learning what you can and can't be flexible with is a life lesson. Whichever end of the "Healthy Boundaries" spectrum you may be, aim to raise the bar.

For example: I certainly don't expect everyone who reads this book to believe everything I believe or share with them. I have learned that I can only share my beliefs from my heart and from my experiences. I trust others to have healthy boundaries and be able to read information perhaps beyond their current knowledge base or comfort zone without feeling threatened.

Related Healthy Habits:
*   #27 Waking Well
*   #35 Grow and Practice Your Faith
*   #40 Encourage

Resources:

*   **The Life You've Always Wanted** by John Ortberg
*   Having Healthy Boundaries – positivelypositive. com/2012/06/29/how-to-create-healthy-boundaries/
*   **Chi-To-Be** book, audio series and coaching By Stacey Hall – chi-to-be.com

Habit 38

Build Your Resource Base

What:

Build a network of go-to resources for various topics in your life. Do not depend on any one source, but create a balanced resource base. This is a collection of reliable books, blogs, people, friends, professionals, products, companies, etc., to seek advice or information from.

Why:

I remember learning about gatekeepers in college. These are the people/companies who control the flow of information in our mainstream world. Now with the internet and the massive information explosion, it is a bigger challenge to control information. This is good news for the discerning student. You have access to many resources, beliefs and information. The ability to discern real health and wisdom from bunk will be your real task.

How To:

- Seek balance in your resources. Have some conservative resources as well as liberal.
- Find resources that reflect real wisdom and value, rather than fad ideas or products.

- Learn to discern. Pray for discernment. Know if a resource is sound or simply bunk.
- Look for 3's. If the resource keeps coming in front of you in significant ways, check it out.
- Realize that some resources are stepping stones for you and others are foundations.
- Recognize when it's time to let go of resources no longer uplifting your quality of life.
- Create resources in various topics like: health; exercise; holistic health; recipes; creative endeavors; relationships.

> **TIP:** Pinterest boards are a great place to do this. You can have public or private boards with links to your resources.

Related Healthy Habits:
- #34 Get Curious/Listen to 3's
- #42 Build a Support System or Support Net

Resources:
- Weston A. Price Foundation – REAL food and REAL health information and resources – westonaprice.org
- Dr. Joseph Mercola – Extensive holistic health information and products – mercola.com
- Dan Burrus – technology trends and wisdom – burrus.com
- The Healthy Habit Coach Blog – thehealthyhabitcoach.com/blog
- Dr. Kaayla Daniel – drkaayladaniel.com
- Body Ecology – information on probiotics, enzymes, recipes and products – bodyecology.com

- Village Green Network – health and REAL food resources – villagegreennetwork.com

---

NOTES:

Habit 39

Become the "Worker Bee"

What:

The "Worker Bee" is an individual who knows their purpose in life, yet is not always able to spend hours at a time on a project, and must work in little pockets or bursts toward the final goal. A necessary skill is to leave the work in a state where it can be picked up again when time and energy permits.

Moms are great examples of worker bees. Whether they are employed outside of the home or not, they are generally the owner/operator of the household. If they are going to get creative or purpose driven projects done (like writing a book), then they need to find skillful ways to work and store the elements and find pockets of time to work. A worker bee is NOT a workaholic. A worker bee has a great work ethic, healthy boundaries, perseverance, a solid sense of values and purpose and is almost always an indispensable force to be reckoned with.

Why:

The worker bee in this case is able to sustainably manage roles and tasks that may not always be glamorous or fun but are necessary. Part of the worker bee's strength lies in the ability to carry out or manage daily tasks while also slowly being able to complete projects that are important aspects of the worker bee's purpose on the planet. Not all worker bee's aspirations are completed in a public arena. Some of the great projects may never even be witnessed by another human being, but they are significant in fulfilling the life purpose intended for the worker bee.

How To:

- Create and Read your mission statement daily and know who you are and where you are going.
- Once you know what goal/project is next, then set about creating an outline.
- Find ways to celebrate little goals along the way.
- Keep the finish line in sight.

Related Healthy Habits:
- #27 Waking Well
- #29 Release, Rest and Rejuvenate
- #37 Create Healthy Boundaries

Resources:

- **Chi-To-Be** book, audio series and coaching By Stacey Hall – chi-to-be.com
- Dr Madohber-Jacobs & Dr. Florence Jameson – Volunteers in Medicine Nevada – vmsn.org
- The Cupcake Girls Las Vegas – thecupcakegirls.org

Habit 40

Encourage Others

What:

Be an uplifting force for people – from your spouse, all the way to people halfway around the world. How you give the encouragement is just as important as what you say to encourage. Your tone can accent or counteract the intention of encouragement.

Why:

There are many events, people and circumstances that threaten to knock the wind out of your sails daily. In contrast, how do you feel when something or someone catches you off guard and creates a smile on your face or laughter in your heart? We all know people who feel energizing to be around. Be one of those people.

How To:

- My chiropractor, Dr. David Hetzel commissioned me to "never become discouraged" and I took that advice to heart. Does that mean I don't have some down days or disappointments that occur? No, of course I'm human and have ups and downs. But when I stay grounded, I am giving and loving. When I am giving and loving, then it is effortless and endless to be able to encourage others.

Related Healthy Habits:

- #42 Build a Support System
- #95 Social Ministry vs. Social Media

Resources:

- **The Book of Psalms** in **the Bible** by God
- **The Different Drum: Community and Making Peace** by M. Scott Peck – mscottpeck.com
- **Fred Factor and Fred 2.0** by Mark Sanborn – marksanborn. com
- **Married for Life** by David C. Cook

Habit 41

Be True to Your Quest

What:

This habit is about knowing who you are, why you are on this planet and honoring that quest. A quest and a mission statement can be, but are not always, one and the same. I think of a quest as the adventure you experience as you move towards a specific end point or goal. The mission statement is not just what you are here to do but who you want to be while doing it.

Being true to your quest involves both of these.

For example: For a long time I knew I wanted to create healthy ripples. Although I knew I wanted to go on this quest, it was very sketchy exactly how I would be going about it. Next, my friend Stacey Hall helped me create my mission statement or B-All and develop a Strategic Attraction Plan. As I created and focused on these, my quest began revealing itself loud and clear. What I've experienced is that as I seek the truth of my purpose on this planet and keep myself healthy and clear, I am able to spend my energy and talent in a direction with great velocity and ease. (Thank you, Stacey, for that term and direction.)

Why:

We all need a sense of purpose in our lives. Even survivors of long term imprisonment will find ways to feel significant by creating a code to communicate with others or by keeping count of days in captivity. This significance does not need to come from some grand journey; it can come from the seemingly smallest act of ongoing kindness. I think of the moms I know who have found their quests by dedicating themselves to caring for ill family members or volunteering once a week to read to the elderly. When your heart is called to a quest, the reward isn't the finish line as much as it is who you have to become in order to accomplish the journey. Being true to that quest is aligning your destination with your character and purpose.

How To:

- Journaling
- Create a mission statement or B-All.
- Create and read your Strategic Attraction Plan Daily (SAP).
- Handwrite Your top 10 goals daily.
- Practice Daily God/Goals time.

Related Healthy Habits:

- #27 Waking Well
- #81 Accountability Responsibility

Resources:

- **The Artist's Way** By Julie Cameron – juliacameronlive.com
- Dr. Leo Buscaglia – buscaglia.com
- Dr. Bernie Seigel – berniesiegelmd.com
- **The Purpose Driven Life** by Rick Warren
- **Chi-To-Be** book, audio series and coaching By Stacey Hall

   – chi-to-be.com

- **Fred Factor and Fred 2.0** by Mark Sanborn – marksanborn. com
- Charlie Plumb – POW Survivor and Proufound Speaker – speaker.charlieplumb.com

---

NOTES:

Habit 42

Build a Support System

What:

A support system or support net is a group of solid "go to" people for you to glean wisdom and moral support from. This differs from Healthy Habit #38 Build a Resource Base in that it tends to be two way and personal communication instead of just gathering information from public figures or holistic health professionals. However, depending on the circles you dance in, you may have friends in both groups. I am VERY grateful for my friends in the Holistic Health Community, Foodie Friends, Fellow Essential Oilers, church family, neighborhood friends and family.

Why:

A Support System or Net is important because sometimes we just need a sounding board, a shoulder or an understanding heart to encourage us. And sometimes we just need a support net to catch us when we occasionally fall.

How To:

- Join like interest groups such as associations, Meetup. com Community Groups, Weston A. Price Foundation Local Chapters, or social media groups.

- Become active by volunteering in a great local church.
- If you keep crossing paths with certain people, maybe you are supposed to be getting to know them better. Invite them out to coffee or for a hike.
- Host a Movie night or potluck.

Related Healthy Habits:
- #38 Build Your Resource Base
- #85 Host a Movie Showing
- #87 Community Unity Potluck
- #98 Be a Fred

Resources:

- Meetup.com – Online message board for local community interest groups.
- Weston A. Price Foundation Local Chapter Groups – westonaprice.org/local-chapters/find-local-chapter
- Find a Willow Creek Association Church in your area – willowcreek.com/membership/membersearch.asp
- Join Healthy Habits Meetup.com Group – meetup.com/HealthyHabitsLasVegas
- Visit Verve in Las Vegas for a mission trip – vivalaverve.org
- **Fred Factor and Fred 2.0** by Mark Sanborn – marksanborn.com

Habit 43

The Cleanse

What:

A cleanse is a practice to rid the body and it's filtering organs of accumulated waste and toxins. There are many types of cleanses and protocols for cleansing. Most people are referring to colon cleansing when they think about this subject. The truth is that there are many types of cleanses: large and small colon cleansing; liver, gallbladder; parasite cleansing; kidney cleansing. You name it, you can likely cleanse it.

If you are trying to do a full body cleanse, please enlist the help of someone skilled in this practice. There is a particular order of cleansing that makes sense to the body. For example, if you have a ton of digestive issues, cleansing the colon might make more sense to do first so that other organs don't dump waste into an already burdened intestinal system.

Why:

Every day we are exposed to massive amounts of toxins (consciously and unconsciously) and have fewer lifestyle activities to help us release these toxins. Many holistic healthcare practitioners believe that disease is the result of toxicity, the accumulation of waste/toxins in the body. With the onslaught of burdens on our bodies and the scarcity of ways to detox, active and regular cleansing is vital to our health and well being. Many people find a relief of chronic issues or experience sustainable weight loss after cleansing.

How To:

- Consult with your doctor about what kind of cleanse you will be doing. Whether you are going to ask permission or not, your doctor is on your team and really needs to be in on the process.
- Work with a practitioner who knows how to support a cleansing person.
- Commit to following the protocol exactly. People have spent years learning why and how to cleanse properly.
- Understand that you might feel pretty lousy as your body detoxes. This is normal. You will feel excellent when you are finished.
- Please do not just quit half way. At that point you have basically stirred up a bunch of junk in your system and if you just quit without allowing it to exit, you could really cause problems with your health.

Related Healthy Habits:
- #2 Manage Your Bucket
- #20 Fasting

Resources:

- **The Complete Master Cleanse and Beyond the Master Cleanse** by Tom Woloshyn
- **The Liver and GallBladder Miracle Cleanse** by Andreas

Moritz
- Learn about colonics and coffee enemas
- Find a Holistic Health Practitioner or Colonic Practitioner

NOTES:

Habit 44

Conscious Posture

What:

According to Dr. Pete Hilgartner, how you sit, sleep and stand every day can be a contributing factor to good health or not. More specifically, we are talking about the posture or positions you sit, sleep and stand and how they can shape your muscles and spinal column. Having good form when you are exercising and performing daily tasks is important in supporting good posture, muscle tone and wellness.

Why:

Passive or poor posture can affect your health in a variety of ways such as muscle tone, respiratory issues, stress and weight gain. Once you become aware of how you sit, stand and sleep, you start to notice what is beneficial for your health or not. If you are unsure, there are great chiropractors, sports medicine experts and physical therapists trained in proper posture and form when you are exercising or performing normal daily tasks.

I had a massage therapist point out to me how much my muscles were revealing about my daily posture. I was showing signs of early humpback – EEEK! He gave me some simple exercises to do to help compensate for the fact that most of my daily activities involved head forward, looking slightly down and shoulders rounding. Hmmm. Cooking. Blogging. Writing books. Creating presentations and products while at my computer. Talking to my kids…listening to my kids. These are all activities involving looking downward. That was a valuable observation for me at a time period when I still had the chance to change my daily posture.

Another important factor was when my friend and master pilates instructor Aleisa George noticed me favoring one side while doing sit ups. I said that I had a strange tailbone that veered off to one side and that I had to compensate for it. She explained how important it was to be balanced and have good form or it might throw my body even more out of whack. I had to be mindful of all the ways I might have been compensating for this seemingly little defect. WOW! What an eyeopening realization. I realized how many ways I'd been compensating or standing, sitting or sleeping in positions because of my issue and throwing myself out of balance.

How To:

- Pay attention to how you are sitting, sleeping and standing. Take note, or set a timer periodically throughout the day and give yourself a posture inventory.
- Notice if your gut is out or tucked in. Are your shoulders back or rounded forward? Do the chairs you sit in mostly encourage or discourage good posture?
- Lose the back of your chair. Seriously. Sitting without your chair back causes you to engage your stomach muscles and sit up straight.
- Schedule a session with a massage therapist, sports medicine

expert or chiropractor to help you discern any issues that might be presenting themselves.

- Be mindful of how you may or may not be compensating or creating poor structural issues.

Related Healthy Habits:
- #50 The Message of the Massage
- #59 Travel Exercise
- #66 Invest in Massages, Steams and Saunas

Resources:
- Hilgartner Health Institute – hilgartnerhealth.com
- Aleisa George with Centerworks Pilates – centerworks.com
- Nia Technique – nianow.com
- Dr. David Hetzel, Henderson, NV – 702-260-1164
- The Nevada Clinic – Las Vegas, NV – nevadaclinic.com
- Relax the Back Store for ergonomically sound chairs.
- Check out my guest editor post call Sitting Well on Caldera Spas 20 Minute Renewal blog – calderaspas.com/en/ health-wellness/20-minute-renewal/2013/01/24/sitting-well-improve-posture-these-10-healthy-habits/

Walk the Talk

What:

Do what you say you are doing. Do what you are asking others to do or being honest about it when you are not. What is important here is twofold.

1. Don't act like the poster child for health who has no faults, weaknesses, bad habits or problems. Be transparent. Sharing your own challenges endears you to people and helps them feel like you are on the same team. Hiding out in the back room with a pint of ice cream isn't congruent and can shoot you in the foot and destroy your credibility.

2. Don't expect perfection from experts or people trying to help others live healthier lives. I'm the first to tell you I am soooo not perfect. I still drink coffee, like sugar way more than I should, have wine occasionally and have kids who want to explore junk food. I am however on the journey alongside you trying to be a better version of myself daily. This book is a roadmap to getting back on course.

Why:

Because nobody wants to listen to someone who is not following their own advice. It feels slimy. Sometimes the biggest voices opposing something, are also the biggest practitioners of exactly what they are opposing.

How To:

- Be transparent. This means fess up when you need to and do your best not to act "holier than thou."
- Create and be a support system rather than a kitchen or exercise police.
- Some people work better with an accountability partner or group. Ultimately, you are accountable to yourself, but some folks like to have help and support from others.
- No shaming or guilt allowed.

Related Healthy Habits:
- #38 Build a Resource Base
- #42 Build a Support System

Resources:

- Your conscience :-D

Habit 46

Create Healthy Traditions

What:

Traditions are activities, habits, foods, celebrations, etc., that we as a culture, a community, family or individual engage in on a regular basis. Although many traditions are cultural and have historical or spiritual significance, there are traditions we can create in our own spheres of influence. What you anchor with a tradition is your choice :-)

Why:

Traditions can be fun and a great way to express fellowship, friendship, political or deep spiritual beliefs. They can tell stories and teach the younger generations important life lessons or ways to celebrate wonderful accomplishments. What traditions do you follow as a family, as a community or in your culture? Are the habits and activities uplifting to your health or a stressor in it? Are there ways to participate and change what isn't uplifting? Is it something you can reframe your anchored associations with? If you don't practice any traditions (there are plenty of people who don't), why not? Why not create or participate in one in your own way and see how it feels?

How To:

You get to choose. You can revisit an established tradition, or create your own. Play. Have fun, create significance for you and your household.

In my house, we have a last day of school tradition – the field trip. It can be a surprise to my kids or a planned event. My kids are oftentimes sad the last day of school because they not only like school but have many friends that will be moving and not coming back the following year. Having this fun family tradition uplifts them and creates memories they will look back on and perhaps continue with their own families one day.

Related Healthy Habits:
- #30 Engage the Whole Family
- #32 The Power of Anchors
- #33 Create Healthy Rewards
- #87 Community Unity Potlucks

Resources:

- Healthy Traditions – pinterest.com/tararayburn/healthy-traditions
- Stay tuned for upcoming book from The Healthy Habit Coach

Habit 47

Be Wise With Your Time

What:

We all have the exact amount of time in one day. What we do with our time can differ dramatically. Being wise with your time isn't measuring how much you can do in a day but rather the quality of what you can do or "not" do in a day. Being wise with your time is about quality not quantity. I look at many countries who seem to honor and protect siestas, vacation and family time. The wisest habits I practice are "Power Naps" and vacations. I can be much more efficient, productive and pleasant when I take that 15-30 minute rest in the afternoon. Just ask my kids ;-) Also, the rejuvenation from vacations completely ground and energize me as well as provide much needed, uninterrupted time with my family.

Why:

Today, we are constantly being wooed for our attention and our time. People have such jam packed schedules they leave very little of what I call "white space" in their day. White space is that blank space that really can allow for God to work and inspiration and rejuvenation to flow in us.

How To:

- Make a flow chart or list of your week to see where you are currently spending your time.
- Review this chart/list to see if it is really how and where you want to be spending time.
- Think in terms of "investing" your time rather than spending. Are the activities and habits well invested or are they like throwing money down the drain?
- Write a personal mission statement or as Stacey Hall calls it a B-All (your be all, end all who you are put here to be) **My B-All:** I am a student of Grace and I inspire uplifting habits for the Mind, Body and Soul.
- Start your day by grounding, focusing on positive thoughts/ words, reading your personal mission statement and handwriting your goals. This keeps you focused on who you are and where you are inspired to be going.
- Leave room for the "white space" or open time and flexibility. Great things happen there.
- Pray for discernment about whether or not an invitation or activity is uplifting or distracting. Not all invitations are wise uses of your time, talent and energy.
- Take vacations.
- Vary vacation's vocation.

Related Healthy Habits:
- #27 Waking Well
- #46 Create Healthy Traditions
- #73 Vary Vacation's Vocation

Resources:

- **The Purpose Driven Life** by Rick Warren

- **The Time is Now, The Person is You** by Nido Qubein
- **Do It Well. Make It Fun** by Ronald P. Culberson
- **Chi-To-Be** book, audio series and coaching By Stacey Hall
  – chi-to-be.com

NOTES:

Habit 48

Focus on the Shoot

What:

This is the idea of focusing on where you want to go, or more importantly, who you want to be. Many people live lives based on fear and focus on the negative events or aspects of life. It is my experience that this practice will get you more of the same – what you spend your time focused on is what you'll get more of.

Why:

This idea came to me when Mike and I used to whitewater kayak. When you were scouting a rapid, there were clearly routes you wanted to be on leading you safely to your intended destination. However, there were also plenty of places on the river you did NOT want to be – like the keeper holes or giant rocks. Once you got back into your kayak to run the rapid, you were commissioned to focus on the shoot (wave tongue) that would assist you in getting to your destination with minimum effort. The challenge here is that it is human nature to want to focus on that ugly, scary place where you "don't" want to be instead. Funny thing happens…your boat will almost always go where you are looking. Look at the shoot and you'll get to where you want to be, look at the rock… and BAM! You will end up hitting the rock.

How To:

- Look clearly at the path you are on. Is it really leading to where you want to go or more importantly where God wants you to go?
- Know where you want to be. A great tool for this is Stacey Hall's energy surges about planning for success in the Chi-To-Be Coaching series and the Strategic Attraction Plan (SAP)
- Practice focusing on your SAP daily. This also involves creating the steps, or as Stacey Hall calls them, the "Intentional Activities" to get to those goals.

Related Healthy Habits:
- #27 Waking Well
- #32 The Power of Anchors
- #47 Be Wise With Your Time
- #92 Off Balance, On Purpose
- #94 See What Isn't There
- #98 Be a Fred

Resources:

- **Chi-To-Be** books, CD's and Coaching by Stacey Hall
- **Attracting the Perfect Customers** by Stacey Hall and Jan Brogniez
- **What IF** keynote speech and book by Mike Rayburn
- **Off Balance, On Purpose** by Dan Thurmon
- **Fred 2.0** by Mark Sanborn
- **The Purpose Driven Life** by Rick Warren
- **The Time is Now The Person is Your** by Nido Qubein
- God/Goal Time Resource at 100EasyHealthyHabits.com

Habit 49

No Stress Eating

What:

Practice habits to reduce and release stress before, during and after meals. This improves health by taking the body out of "fight or flight" mode and supports good hormone function and allows for focus on proper digestion and good absorption of nutrients.

Why:

Stress lowers immune system, impedes digestion, slams the endocrine system, hinders absorption and can set the stage for a host of other issues. If you create a "stress-less" meal time, you will create habits that support your wellness. Even the most nutrient rich foods aren't utilized well by a stressed-out body.

How To:

- Take 3 Deep Breaths before you begin to eat.
- Chew, Chew, Chew.
- Avoid talking with your mouth full. (My bad habit – Eek!)
- No matter how small the nibble or meal, use a dish or a bowl.
- Keep uplifting choices handy.
- Sit while you eat. This sets the body up to digest better by coming out of fight or flight mode.

- No electronics at the table.
- Turn the TV and other media sources off at mealtime.
- No high energy/busy/loud or music some members do not like. All should be in agreement for music choice or it goes off.
- Avoid answering phones/doorbells/texts/e-mails etc., if at all humanly possible during mealtime.
- Release guilt. If you make a less than uplifting choice, then bless it and move on.

Related Healthy Habits:
- #2 Manage Your Bucket
- #8 Digestion Suggestions
- #23 Chew, Chew, Chew

Resources:
- The Healthy Habit Coach Blog – thehealthyhabitcoach.com/blog
- The Healthy Home Economist – theHealthyHomeEconomist.com
- Kelly the Kitchen Kop – KellytheKitchenKop.com
- Chef Shane Kelly – chefshanekelly.com
- Nutritionist Dr. Lolin Hilgartner – hilgartnerhealth.com

Habit 50

The Message of The Massage

What:

Your body tells a story. Your daily posture helps write that story. Is your posture writing a health and wellness story, a comedy or a horror story? Seriously. The last massage I had revealed how much I have been engaged in activities that cause me to sit, looking down with shoulder slightly slumped forward. EEK! I started realizing that my daily activities (cooking, writing, talking to kids, etc) are causing me to be writing "The Humpback of Notre Dame." ;-)

Why:

Massage is a great tool for relieving stress, detoxing the body, easing aches and pains as well as it is an amazing gift of touch. I am constantly reminded how necessary "appropriate touch" is to our well being. I've been blessed to have massaged feet all over the world and the most striking reaction is not to the pain relieving aspect, but to the real human touch given from a loving place with no ulterior motives.

Some Benefits of Massage

- Physical and Emotional Stress Relief
- Increased blood circulation
- Assists in Detoxification
- Stimulates the lymph system, our body's defense system for toxins
- Appropriate touch is a basic human need

How To:

- Offer to swap massages with family members.
- Go to the local massage school for special pricing or free massages.
- Find the massage kiosks at the mall or airport.
- Schedule a regular massage or Raindrop Technique Experience.

Related Healthy Habits:
- #2 Manage Your Bucket
- #44 Conscious Posture
- #66 Invest in Massage, Steams and Saunas

Special Thanks to massage therapist Paul Lofgreen, CMT, LMT for gently pointing out the issues of my posture and giving me exercises to change the error of my ways ;-)

Resources:

- The Benefits of Massage – massagetherapy.com/articles/index.php?article_id=468
- The Power of Touch – creationhealth.com
- For List of Raindrop Technique Certified Therapists Worldwide – raindroptraining.com

- To Learn Raindrop Technique – raindroptraining.com or
- Purchase Gary Young's Raindrop DVD – lifesciencepublishers. com

NOTES:

"When health is absent, wisdom cannot reveal itself,
art cannot manifest, strength cannot fight,
wealth becomes useless and intelligence
cannot be applied."

Herophilus
- Greek physician (335-280 BC)

Healthy Habits for the Road

Introduction

This section is the fruit of being married to a "Road Warrior" as well as having shared many of the journey's alongside Mike. It is dedicated to my many friends in the National Speakers Association and The Speaker's Roundtable. Traveling for a living is not all glitz and glamour as most people see it. It can be very challenging to practice consistent healthy habits while on the road. In fact, if left unchecked, this lifestyle can be detrimental to your health.

There are more world travelers today than ever which brings both blessings and challenges. 100 Healthy Habits is a springboard for learning about those challenges, and implementing healthy habits for proactively investing in longterm health as a Road Warrior. These habits are great whether you travel for a living or just travel for vacations. Healthy Habits for the Road are sustainable tools for your wellness on the road.

"For God's Temple is Holy and You are that Temple."

1 Corinthians 3:17

Habit 51

Start Strong

What:

Build in nutrient rich anchors and the time to practice uplifting habits before you travel. If you practice healthy habits at least 80% of the time, chances are you are stacking the odds in your health's favor. However, if you travel for a living, it may be very difficult to follow that 80:20 rule. Practicing habits for dialing in daily probiotics, digestive enzymes, nutrient rich foods and beverages and regular exercise at home is critical to building a strong foundation. When the foundation is strong, then the wildcards on the road don't take as much of a toll on your health.

Why:

What you do every day affects your health in exponential ways. Your body will feel the accumulation of switching time zones often, sedentary long flights, eating fast food or skipping meals all together on a regular basis. These habits can age you prematurely and set your body up for chronic issues if you do not learn ways to compensate for "road ways." When you are at home it is critical to practice healthy habits as consistently as possible so that you can compensate for the road hazards you might encounter.

How To:

- Listen to 100 Easy Healthy Habits audio coaching series and read ALL of the Healthy Habits with the intent to find ways to build in the foundation principles in section 1 Healthy Habits for Life as much as possible.
- Be creative in how you tailor the concepts of this section and the whole book for your unique situation.
- Plan your time wisely and don't run yourself ragged right before traveling. Your immune system is a target if you are exhausted and not eating well.

Related Healthy Habits:

- #3 Nutrient Rich Anchors
- #3 Be ProBiotic
- #8 Digestion Suggestions
- #47 Be Wise with Your Time
- #59 Travel Exercise

Resources:

- 100 Easy Healthy Habits Audio Coaching Series and Book.
- **Essential Gluten-Free Recipes** by Tara Rayburn and Mary Vars
- **Healthy Healing** by Linda Page, PhD

Habit 52

Pre-Travel Habits

What:

The daily habits you practice will set you up for success or not. You can amp up your habits prior to travel and stack the deck on your side so that, if you have a lot of travel ups, downs and variables, your system will be strong.

Why:

We experience more variables and unexpected circumstances when we travel than when we are at home. I call these wildcards. Whether it is eating foods that don't uplift you, not getting enough rest or just the stress of travel logistics, these can challenge our systems.

How To:

- Create a list of your nutrient rich anchors and make sure to have the items for the trip.
- Build in exercise and rest time before your trip.
- Take a few minutes to see if there is a gym or community center near where will be staying.
- If you are going to be traveling in a country other than your own, plan to do a parasite cleanse after you get back. Good

parasite cleanses will be 3 weeks on, 1 week off and repeat for 3 cycles. This is to knock out each stage of a parasite's life (egg, youth and adult).

- Bring digestive supporting elements like enzymes or essential oils like Di-Gize or Peppermint.
- Be vigilant in getting your probiotics nightly.
- Take digestive enzymes or consume digestive supportive foods and beverages.

Related Healthy Habits:

- #4 Be Probiotic
- #2 Manage Your Bucket
- #3 Nutritional Anchors
- #8 Digestion Suggestions
- #43 The Cleanse
- #70 Post Travel Cleansing

Resources:

- Vitacost Online is an online resource for many of your health supporting items – vitacost.com
- Young Living – Therapeutic Grade Essential Oils , Quality personal care products and Diffusers – YoungLiving.com *Note: if you already work with a Young Living Distributor, please honor that relationship for ordering. If you are not currently working with a distributor or you are interested in becoming one, please see my website or see Resources in the back of the book.
- To find your local Farmer's Market – localharvest.org
- **Parafree** by Young Living is a good one – Youngliving.org
- Juice Plus+ is another good whole food nutritional supportive anchor. - TheHealthyHabitCoach.com

Knock out the Worst First!

What:

When preparing for a trip, do the task you dislike the most first!

Why:

If you are like me, there is always one task I dislike most in preparing for a trip. Whether the trip is business or pleasure, packing my own clothes is my least favorite task. If I wait until last to do this, I usually end up forgetting something major or harbor a dull, nagging, oppressive stress the whole time I'm prepping for the trip. Sounds silly, but if I hit this task first, the rest of prep time is a joy.

How To:

* Make a good list about a week before your trip so you can add/delete from it as you need to. Keep it handy whether it's on paper or electronic device. If you travel often, it might be good to keep it on your computer so you have a basic framework to work from for each trip.

- A list also reduces anxiety about forgetting something important.
- Once it is time to pack, simply "knock out the worst, first."
- This principle works in reverse too for unpacking.

Related Healthy Habits:
- #54 Healthy Anchors Checklist
- #55 Essential Oil Checklist

Resources:
- Paper & pen ;-D

Habit 54

Healthy Anchors Checklist

What:

This is a list of your "big bang for your buck" health items, specific to travel. The list is good to do a week or two out before longer trips so you have time to purchase any items prior to departure. Since you will be traveling, these items will generally be, but are not always, supplements of some kind although packing healthy snacks for the airplane would qualify.

Why:

As you remember, Healthy/Nutritional Anchors are items or even practices that prove to support your longterm health. When traveling there are some that will prove to keep you supported well before, during and after your trip. If you are unsure where to start, see my list below to help you create your own.

Here are some of the Healthy Anchors for my family:
- Whole food nutritional supplements
- Probiotic supplements that do not need to be refrigerated

- Fermented Cod Liver Oil capsules
- Digestive Enzymes specific to each of the travelers. My son and I use different enzymes than my husband and daughter.
- Digestive distress support such as peppermint essential oil or Di-Gize Blend essential oil
- Therapeutic grade essential oils targeted for particular trip (i.e.: cold and flu season, air quality issues, fatigue, digestion)
- If it is spring or if there are air quality issues where I'm going, I will pack one or more of the following: nasal inhalers, cool mist diffuser, neti pot, sea salt and essential oils for respiratory support.

These have proven themselves to be priceless investments for healthy travels.

How To:

- Make a nuts and bolts list from top priority to "it would be nice to bring."
- Do an inventory to be sure you have enough of these supplies on hand for your trip and for a few days after your return.

Related Healthy Habits:

- #3 Nutritional Anchors
- #4 Be Probiotic
- #8 Digestion Suggestions
- #53 Knock Out the Worst First
- #55 Essential Oil Checklist
- #60 Make the Quart Count

TRAVEL TIP: Know where you are going and what the country's customs are. Many states and countries have different rules and may or may not allow seeds, fruits, herbs, etc., across the border.

Resources:

- Shopping Guide from Weston A. Price Foundation – westonaprice.org – look under order materials
- Your local health food store
- Vitacost for low cost supplements and quick delivery – vitacost.com
- Fermented Cod Liver Oil pills – greenpasture.org
- Cool Mist Diffusers – diffuserworld.com or get a discount and order from link on thehealthyhabitcoach.com/blog
- Homeopathy – Joette Calabrese – joettecalabrese.com or your Integrative Medical Team
- Essential Oils and Supplements – Young Living – Therapeutic Grade Essential Oils , Quality personal care products and Diffusers – YoungLiving.com *Note: if you already work with a Young Living Distributor, please honor that relationship for ordering. If you are not currently working with a distributor or you are interested in becoming one, please see my website or see Resources in the back of the book.

Habit 55

Essential Oil Checklist

What:

This is a collection of three to five therapeutic grade essential oils specific for your journey. Essential Oils are distilled plants that have been used in supporting health for centuries around the world. It is important to "know your farmer" so to speak and how they grow, harvest and distill their oils. You want therapeutic grade oils without fillers and junk ingredients.

Example of a basic essential oil support list:
- Thieves Oil Blend for immune system support and oral hygiene
- Peppermint for digestive support, headaches or natural breath freshening
- Di-Gize Oil Blend for extreme digestive support
- Lavender or Peace and Calming Blend for stress relief and relaxation. Lavender is also good for burns and ear aches.
- Purification Essential Oil Blend for sanitizing cuts, scrapes and insect bites
- Raven or R.C. Essential Oil Blends for respiratory support

Why:

Essential Oils and herbs were once used widely all over the world for health support. They are stable (won't spoil), compact and travel well. I have filled my quart sized bag with essential oils, especially when I am concerned about possibly losing my luggage.

How To:

If you know where you are going, what you will be doing and any seasonal challenges possible, you can start creating a list. There are many essential oils reference books and if you already work with a Young Living Distributor they can help you find resources or create your own list. See my example list above as a starting place.

Related Healthy Habits:
- #54 Healthy Anchors Checklist
- #56 Know Your Challenges
- #63 Sinus Awareness

Resources:

- Young Living – Therapeutic Grade Essential Oils , Quality personal care products and Diffusers – YoungLiving.com *Note: if you already work with a Young Living Distributor, please honor that relationship for ordering. If you are not currently working with a distributor or you are interested in becoming one, please see my website or see Resources in the back of the book.
- **Essential Oils Desk Reference** or **Pocket Guide** by Life Science Publishing – lifesciencepublishers.com
- Essential Oils Travel cases – Abundant Health – abundanthealth4u.com
- Do not purchase cheap oils. Cheap oils get cheap results – or worse. Trust me; I speak from very painful experience.

Habit 56

Know Your Challenges

What:

Know what you and your other travel companion's health concerns or challenges are. Are there issues like allergies, diabetes or other special dietary considerations? Are there physical limitations like high blood pressure, chemical sensitivities, immobility or asthma? Are there any phobias, addictions, depression or emotional situations for everyone to be aware of?

Why:

Having information like this for yourself and for your fellow travel companions in advance allows you all to be proactive in what you pack. If you have sinus issues and snore and tell your roommates, they can proactively pack earplugs.

Knowing your challenges, preparing and sharing in advance also limits the "holy cow factor." The holy cow factor is when one individual has a habit or issue that completely conflicts with others in the group. For example, if one person uses a lot of scented personal care products and the roommate has asthma or is chemically sensitive – there is a potentially life threatening situation here that can be avoided.

How To:

- Simply make a list of your own health challenges or concerns and, if traveling with others, ask them to do the same. Share your lists.
- Proactively pack supplies to support these challenges.
- If you have respiratory issues and you are traveling to a different area in the spring, then packing sinus and lung supportive supplies is being well prepared.

Related Healthy Habits:
- #3 Nutritional Anchors
- #4 Be Probiotic
- #8 Digestion Suggestions
- #53 Knock Out the Worst First
- #55 Essential Oil Checklist
- #60 Make the Quart Count
- #54 Healthy Anchors Checklist

Resources:

- **Healthy Healing** by Linda Page
- The Healthy Habit Coach Blog – thehealthyhabitcoach.com/blog

Habit 57

Do Your Homework - Preparation Saves Perspiration

What:

With a little advanced homework, you can deduce your unique travel challenges and build in anchors to support those particular challenges.

For example, if you are going to a convention, you know that chances will be, 1) Sedentary much of the time, 2) Be in close quarters with large amounts of people, 3) Eating foods you may not be very used to, 4) Tempted to snack on junk food, 5) Needing to drink lots of water to stay hydrated.

Quick List of Proactive Measures to Support You on this Trip:
1. Work in workouts, stretching, deep breathing, practice conscious posture.

2. Pack and use Healthy Anchors, Essential Oils.

3. Make time to rest.

4. Pack nutrient rich snacks.

5. Bring a stainless steel or glass water bottle.

Simple! Do-Able! ;-D

Why:

This small amount of preparation in advance can save you in potential "Hazardous Health" challenges throughout your trip. Being well is being "proactive" instead of "reactive" with your daily habits.

How To:

Find a contact person in the area you are going to be traveling to. If it's for business, get the information from the organizer. If it is a resort or travel destination, find the number for the concierge. Ask questions like: Are there any environmental issues in the area? Is it a safe area to go out walking or jogging? Is there a gym or exercise facility nearby? Is there a grocery store or health food store near?

Related Healthy Habits:
*   #3 Nutritional Anchors
*   #4 Be Probiotic
*   #8 Digestion Suggestions
*   #53 Knock Out the Worst First
*   #55 Essential Oil Checklist
*   #60 Make the Quart Count
*   #54 Healthy Anchors Checklist

Resources:

- Contact person for the event or location you are traveling to
- The Internet for maps, weather, events, reviews, etc.

NOTES:

Habit 58

Pack In Power

What:

Ha! Let's have fun and play with the various ways we can look at this habit.

Literal Power – Pack in power means pack your plugs for your electronic devices, and don't forget to bring them home again too.

Spiritual Power – Pack in power by bringing and practicing your daily spiritual habits such as devotional, journal, Bible.

Emotional Power – Pack in power with your grounding anchors such as journals, books, essential oils or favorite music.

Nutritional Power – Means packing "big bang for the buck" nutrient rich foods, beverages and supplements.

Why:

You improve your health when you bring the power packed elements or tools of the uplifting habits you have at home to "be well." Sometimes just one or two of these can be enough to keep your energy high and healthy while traveling.

How To:

- IPads, smart phones, computer, Kindles are great for storing all of your devotionals, reading and even journaling.

- Pack a few baggies with nutrient rich snacks in them. If you have a sweet tooth, find a healthy sweet treat that won't send your blood sugar skyrocketing but will still satisfy.

Related Healthy Habits:

- #1-100 :-D

Resources:

- 100 Easy Healthy Habits Audio Series and Book by Tara Rayburn. Seriously, I created this series to help you brainstorm this habit of "Packing in Power"
- The Healthy Habit Coach Blog – for ongoing power packed tools and practices – theHealthyHabitCoach.com

Travel Exercise - Travelcise

What:

This habit is loosely defined as creating movement, improving strength, flexibility and circulation. Create ways to increase circulation for your blood and your lymphatic system through movement and deep breathing. Practice daily travelcise for strengthening and toning muscles through weight resistance and challenging specific muscle groups.

Why:

Because if you don't use it, you lose it. REALLY. People who travel a lot for a living go from 1-60 MPH a few times on any given day. They also tend to sit, stand and move in very repetitive ways, (i.e., Carrying computer bag the same way, sleeping positions, sitting at the computer). This repetition can overwork certain muscles and neglect others which sets a body up for structural issues.

How To:

- Create a toolbox of "travelcises" you can practice on the

road that covers all of your muscle groups. Enlist the help of a trainer if you need to or search online.

- **Airplane Travel** – Get up and walk once an hour on long flights. Periodically point, flex toes and roll ankles.
- **Car Travel** – Vary the positions you are in as much as possible. Share the driving with another. Plan rest stops every 2-3 hours. Drink plenty of water.

- Search online for tips, tricks and new exercises.

Related Healthy Habits:
- #21 Exercise as a Habit
- #44 Conscious Posture

Resources:
- Oxycise – Deep breathing and isometrics – oxycise.com
- Nia Technique Fitness – nianow.com
- Qi Gong – Google resources online of find a local class
- P90X – home exercise program – beachbody.com

Make the Quart Count

What:

At the time of this writing most US based flights require you to put any liquid items you are carrying onboard in a quart size plastic bag. Bottle sizes must be under 3 ounces. With a little foresight, you can pack that bag wisely just for the health of it ;-)

Why:

I like to pack my quart size bag with a punch. I usually have peppermint and Thieves essential oils (see #55), my basic non-toxic make-up (in case my luggage gets lost), lip balm, and if it's a long flight, a high energy healthy liquid packet like Young Living's NingXia Red.

How To:

- Use a freezer bag if possible or pack extra baggies for return flight.
- If your essential oils have a child resistant cap, exchange if for a normal one so it doesn't leak.
- You can also use snack size baggies to put essential oils into within the quart size bag to minimize leakage damage.
- If you have skin sensitivities, it's worth packing travel sizes of

your basic personal care products.

Related Healthy Habits:
* #54 Healthy Anchors Checklist
* #55 Essential Oil Checklist

Resources:
* NinqXia Red packets and essential oils from Young Living – youngliving.com

Habit 61

Car Traveling Tips

What:

You have the luxury and flexibility to pack in much more power when you are traveling by automobile. You also have the ability to dial in extra time for stopping and stretching, exercising, or taking a rest break or nap. These are all great for keeping you healthier on the road. Even fun stops at crazy roadside attractions can reduce stress and support whole body health. I'll never forget the Boggy Creek Monster in Fouke, Arkansas.

Why:

You are building health when you practice circulation, hydration, rest and breaks with REAL food instead of engage in long periods with coffee, junk food and monotony.

How To:

- Use various sized ice chests/coolers, small for easy access to snacks, large for basic supplies if you are going to have access to a kitchen.
- Pack learning and inspirational audios and uplifting music to keep your mind active.
- Practice Deep Breathing and Isometrics while driving.

- Pack freezer bags for making ice packs.

Related Healthy Habits:

- #9 Eat REAL Food
- #59 Travelcise

Resources:

- Cooler – varied sizes are good and wheels on the biggest cooler
- Roadside Attraction Finder – roadsideamerica.com

Habit 62

Build In Downtime
on The Road

What:

Build in downtime or white space while you are on your trip. This can range from time set aside for a 30 minute Power Nap to choosing to build in an extra day of travel so you don't have to pull a red-eye flight.

Why:

Your bucket can quickly become too full when you are on constant fight or flight mode. It's easy to become overloaded while visiting in completely different environments and eating foods you may not be used to eating. Building in downtime is time invested in living well. Whether it is for physical rest, mental release or just plan laughter, it uplifts your mind, body and soul.

Another great perk for building in downtime is that it will oftentimes spark creativity, help you arrive at a solution or simply rejuvenate your spirit.

How To:

- Make time to rest daily. Even a 15 minute Power Nap can reset and rejuvenate your system.
- Plan an outing like going to a show, a museum or renting bikes.
- Find a local venue to go pray and practice your faith. Honestly, I don't even think it matters what faith the venue is as long as they are welcoming and willing to allow you to respectfully be present with God and not participate if something is incongruent with your faith. Best if you can find a service or place consistent with your faith.
- Find out if there is a yoga, Nia or Tai Chi class in the area.
- Take 20 minute daily walks.

Related Healthy Habits:
- #29 Release, Rest and Rejuvenate
- #47 Be Wise with Your Time
- #31 Eat, Sleep, Drink – Ms. Mary's Mantra

Resources:

- Become a student of rest and creative downtime

Habit 63

Sinus Awareness

What:

Practicing good habits for your sinuses is an excellent proactive healthy habit. Your sinuses take a huge beating when you travel. Regardless of whether or not you have allergies, there are noxious toxins in our air on massive levels. During travel you may find yourself in small people-packed places with rather stagnant air quality. The quality of our food can also affect our sinuses creating excess mucous or inflammation. Consuming too much sugar, chemicals, dyes and preservatives can also wreak havoc in our airways. Genetically Modified Organisms in our foods pose an unpredictable wildcard for issues and symptoms whose outcome nobody can predict.

Why:

Have you ever really looked at an air conditioner filter when it is exchanged for a fresh one? It's pretty disgusting. Can you imagine what your sinuses may look like after just one spring or after years of living in an air quality challenged area?

How To:

Neti Pot: Be proactive and when you are in areas of high pollen, poor air quality or it's flu season, use a neti pot once or twice a day. Use slightly warm, spring water and sea salt. If you are already experiencing congestion or inflammation, definitely do this twice a day and at least 1/2 hour before bed to allow for drainage. (Google How to Videos for using the Neti Pot or go to see my post – thehealthyhabitcoach.com/health-and-wellness/ spring-allergy-support.)

Nostril Swabbing: Swab your nostrils with a mixture of castor or olive oil and a tiny pinch of Purification blend essential oil in the morning and at night especially after using a neti pot. It coats and protects your nostrils and traps pollens too.

Nasal Inhalers: You can make your own nasal inhaler with essential oils and purchasing empty nasal inhalers (they make plastic or metal versions). Some of my favorite combinations are: Peppermint/Lemongrass, Lemon/Frankincense, R.C. or Raven Blends, Peace and Calming or Sacred Frankincense.

Cool Mist Diffusing: I prefer Cool Mist diffusers that are metal and glass. These great tools infuse the air with tiny particles of therapeutic grade essential oils for sanitizing and supporting healthy sinuses and respiratory systems. They are not plug in or heating the oils in any way. You can even plug them into an appliance timer so they go off periodically throughout the day. I also like the Aria by Young Living for my son who deals with lung issues. It uses water vapor to disperse oils into the air and is better than any humidifier in my opinion.

Deep Breathing-Sinus Specific Exercises: These are designed to promote circulation, good oxygen intake and the releasing of toxins from your lungs and sinus cavities. You can go online or explore books written with plenty of practices to choose from.

Nutrient Rich, Organic, Non-GMO Foods: Wheat and dairy products can aggravate sinus issues by creating excess mucous and inflammation. By supplying the body with easy to digest, nutrient rich foods you give it the necessary tools it needs to build a strong immune system. Soups and broths are some of my favorite ways to infuse the body with nutrients.

Related Healthy Habits:
- #15 Nasal Hygiene
- #64 Hotel Hygiene

Resources:
- Bloomin' Allergy Support post by The Healthy Habit Coach – thehealthyhabitcoach.com/health-and-wellness/bloomin-allergy-support
- Baraka ceramic neti pots – sinussupport.com
- Cool Mist Diffusers available from DiffuserWorld.com or Order from link on thehealthyhabitcoach.com/blog
- **Essential Gluten-Free Recipes** for soup and broth recipes – thehealthyhabitcoach.com/books/essential-gluten-free-recipes
- Nasal Inhalers at abundanthealth4u.com or LivingAnnointed.com
- Purification Blend Essential Oil by Young Living – Therapeutic Grade Essential Oils , Quality personal care products and Diffusers – YoungLiving.com *Note: if you already work with

a Young Living Distributor, please honor that relationship for ordering. If you are not currently working with a distributor or you are interested in becoming one, please see my website or see Resources in the back of the book.

- Sea Salt – the more color the more nutrients present – available at most health food stores
- Castor oil or Olive oil available at most health food stores or online

Habit 64

Hotel Hygiene

What:

You can travel with a few items for supporting your health without chemicals and practice easy habits for Hotel Hygiene. Hotels, motels, resorts and condos all have one thing in common: a lot of people circulate through these living spaces in a short amount of time. Our culture typically resorts mostly to bug blasting with heavy chemicals for "sanitizing" these environments.

Why:

Heavy chemicals can burden our system with toxins that wreak havoc with our endocrine system (our hormones). The challenge is also that these chemical cleaners do not necessarily kill all pathogens (bacteria, fungus, parasites, etc.) and give people a false sense of security.

How To:

- Carry a small bottle of natural sanitizing, safe for spraying on bed, pillows suitcases, shower and bath area, etc. I use a small glass spray bottle with colloidal silver and a few drops of Purification Blend or peppermint or lavender essential oil.
- Pull back the bedcover before lying down on the bed. Even

in nice hotels, these hardly get washed.

- Bring your own water bottle and purchase spring water in a gallon size or more before checking into your hotel.
- Pack a travel size or cool mist diffuser for air quality and respiratory support.
- Bring your own toiletries.
- Pack flip flops for wearing in the shower. Wet, dark moist places harbor germs even after a cleaning.
- Pack slippers or wear flip flops. Avoid walking barefoot if possible.

Related Healthy Habits:
- #63 Sinus Awareness

Resources:

- Cool Mist Diffusers available from DiffuserWorld.com or get a discount and order from link on thehealthyhabitcoach.com/blog
- Small glass spray bottles – abundanthealth4u.com
- Young Living – Therapeutic Grade Essential Oils , Quality personal care products and Diffusers – YoungLiving.com *Note: if you already work with a Young Living Distributor, please honor that relationship for ordering. If you are not currently working with a distributor or you are interested in becoming one, please see my website or see Resources in the back of the book.

Habit 65

Healthy Requests

What:

If you are traveling for business or pleasure, you may have opportunities to make healthy requests that support your health and wellness while traveling. Just ask. Worst thing you could hear is "no" and the best you can hear is "sure." We can also make healthy requests of our clients or business associates paying for our accommodations.

Why:

The more we as a culture request healthy options or pay to stay with hotels that offer them, the more the hospitality industry will listen and perhaps make them commonplace. For example, request to stay at a hotel that has a gym or a healthy place to eat. Ask if they have natural toiletries or cleaning supplies. Many more people are becoming chemically sensitive, so the more we ask, the more they might listen.

How To:

- If you suspect or have been asked about a "goodie basket," request a fruit basket instead of a "Junk Food" basket (you might want to word that a bit nicer).

- Request accommodations with a gym, sauna or steam room.

Related Healthy Habits:
- #18 Personal Care Product Purification
- #84 Make Your Own Skin Care Products

Resources:

- 100 Easy Healthy Habits audio Coaching Series and book
- Environmental Working Group – ewg.org
- Dr. Joseph Mercola's blog/newsletter – mercola.com

Habit 66

Invest in Massages, Steams or Saunas

What:

Massages, steams and saunas all help flush the body of toxins, support the immune system and assist with a general sense of wellbeing. These are habits invested in longterm wellness.

Why:

We are being exposed to more chemicals every day than our grandparents were exposed to in their whole lifetimes. Nobody really knows how all of those chemicals are going to affect our bodies. We do know that many of those elements stick around our body and need active detoxification. Perspiration and circulation are great ways to detox.

How To:

- Make a healthy request that you stay in a hotel offering one or more of these services.
- You might add you are willing to pay for them but that they help you stay well on the road.

- Find out if there is a good spa near your accommodations while traveling.
- Purchase and pack a hand-held, heated body massager.
- Bring a body brush to practice dry brushing in the morning and evening or before showers.

Related Healthy Habits:
- #50 The Message of the Massage

Resources:

- Wellness Travel and Spa Finder – spafinder.com
- Become a member of a chain fitness center who typically has these services and find out how to utilize their locations while you travel. YMCA's are usually great about this and usually have free or minimal fee access to their locations.

Habit 67

Be Present While Away

What:

Many people travel for a living or live away from family and friends. Practicing habits for connection and keeping a presence in your household or circle of friends is crucial to maintaining healthy relationships. I love the ability we now have with cell phones and computers to stay connected with our family members who travel or live elsewhere. Yes, the argument against EMF emissions is valid, but there are always trade-offs in life.

There are also simple non-electronic ways to "Be Present While Away," like hiding notes to be discovered with encouraging words or arranging for little surprises to appear while you are gone. The important element with any of these habits is to foster and fuel connection.

Why:

When a family member or friend travels a lot or works unusual hours, they end up missing out on day to day basic activities, as well as some of the major milestones in our loved ones' life from time to time. Finding ways to keep connected or to express care and affection when you are not present is priceless to those we care about. Sometimes just a text to say, "hi, I'm thinking about you" or "how was your day" can be a little lift in that person's day.

The joy and connection I have experienced from Mike and I being able to text, share photos, Skype with each other and our kids while we travel has been life changing. I married someone who will always travel. I knew from the beginning that it was not only part of his life's work, but that it was a part of him. There are many people engaging in worldwide travel, so practicing habits to stay present and connected while away are vital for maintaining healthy relationships.

How To:

- Hide a few little notes, jokes, etc., around the house to be found while you are away.
- Set a daily timer to stop and check in with a call, a text or even a prayer.
- Take pictures of funny people, places or events on your travels and text them or post them on a public or private Pinterest Board or your Instagram account, or create private slideshows to post or send links to loved ones.
- Give affirmations and heartfelt compliments to express gratitude to friends and family.
- Bring samples of beach sand, photos of local roadside attractions, recorded messages sent via text messaging or e-mail.
- Record bedtime stories that your kids can listen to when you are gone for long trips.

Related Healthy Habits:

- #30 Engage the Whole Family
- #40 Encourage
- #46 Create Healthy Traditions

Resources:

- Apple Stores for multimedia training – apple.com
- Pinterest for creating board for sharing with your friends and family -pinterest.com/tararayburn
- Instagram – another photo sharing App – instagram.com/ healthyhabits

Habit 68

Business as Usual?

What:

What is business as usual in your home? Is it being gone most of the time or for long periods of time? The world works in mysterious ways these days. The internet and webinars have transformed the workplace, and business as usual in your home can look very different than ten years ago. I believe it will look even more interesting in another ten years. The options to travel more and farther or to run the show from your kitchen table are endless.

Perhaps you work from home. My husband and I are self employed doing what we love doing…work days could easily roll into work nights and weekends depending on what projects or events we are in the midst of. Many people work from home now which can be a blessing and a curse at the same time. Great no commute time, unusual work hours and days…not so great. There can be a real blur between business hours and family time. I encourage you and your family to "Create Healthy Boundaries" in the home and on the road.

Why:

I used to write blogs and work on books in the kitchen beside my kids thinking to myself "hey, at least I'm with them." Well, the reality is from their perspective, I'm not really present. I'm engrossed in my work in their home space and not interacting with them. That is just as challenging, if not more, than being halfway around the world on a business trip.

Worldwide business hours are another factor for consideration here. When doing business with people in different time zones, scheduling calls or video conferences at 2am from the home office can really be disruptive to the rest of the household. It can also be difficult to call loved ones from the road at appropriate times for each party. Set some ground rules for alternate times and ways to communicate.

How To:

- Have defined business hours as much as possible and know your values and their priority. For me it is: God, Mike, kids, family and friends, career. I'd love to say that they always actually are practiced in that order, but things happen. I do try and compensate for when that does and build in extra time for the slighted priority. (see habit # 92 Off Balance on Purpose)
- If I have a radio or Skype interview at a time when the kids are home, I let them know in advance and even had my daughter create a sign for my door "On Air...Shhhh ;-)"
- Rethink your career often. Is it conducive to a strong family or relationship? If not, can new uplifting habits transform it to be? Are you gone too much? Are you home too much?
- Does your family have a positive anchor associated with your career or not? What can you do to change or improve that?
- Do your best not to answer e-mails and text messages during defined family time.

Related Healthy Habits:
- #37 Have Healthy Boundaries
- #40 Encourage
- #47 Be Wise with Your Time
- #67 Be Present While Away
- #92 Off Balance on Purpose – Dan Thurmon

Resources:
- The Entrepreneur's Source Blog – entrepreneurssource.com/blog.html
- Stacey Hall and the **Chi-To-Be** books, audios and movement – chi-to-be.com
- **Off Balance on Purpose** by Dan Thurmon – danthurmon.com/off-balance-on-purpose

Make Your Beverages Count

What:

Choose beverages that uplift your health and wellness rather than slowly degenerate it. Drinks, juices and smoothies can be rich sources of probiotics, enzymes, minerals and other detoxification and nourishing goodies. One of the main causes of headaches I witness more often than not is simple dehydration. Replenishing with bountiful beverages energizes you.

Why:

Beverages can boost your health or be silent stalkers of good health. Many people don't really "count" what they do or don't drink daily. When I ask for food diaries most people leave out what they are and are not drinking daily. Just one can of regular soda has about 40 grams of sugar, lowers your immune system for hours and sends your body into sugar crash in just one hour. WOW! Don't know about you, but I sure don't want to choose a wildcard like that for my health. (Search Mercola.com for "What Happens to Your Body Within an Hour of Drinking a Coke.")

How To:

- Pack a stainless steel or glass water bottle to bring. You'll drink more healthy beverages, be able to add essential oils to them and not be ingesting toxins or creating waste from plastic bottles.
- Pack herbal tea bags and a mason jar for making sun tea in your hotel window during the day so you have a bountiful beverage when you get back to the room.
- Bring a packet of probiotic powder to add to your drink at night.
- Bring Stevia with you instead of using toxic artificial sweeteners.
- Find a juice bar and explore flavors like sour, bitter & spicy. Too many people load up on sugar in smoothies thinking they are doing something good for their bodies.

Related Healthy Habits:
- #4 Be Probiotic
- #8 Digestion Suggestions
- #31 Eat, Sleep, Drink – Ms. Mary's Mantra

Resources:

- **Essential Gluten-Free Recipes 2nd Edition** by Tara Rayburn and Mary Vars. Check out the Bountiful Beverage section for great recipes for uplifting nutrient rich beverages.
- Dr. OhHira's Professional Formula Probiotics – harvestmoonhealthfoods.com
- PRObiotic 225 from Ortho Molecular Products
- Mountain Rose Herbs – for bulk herbs and herbal teas – mountainroseherbs.com
- Bloomin' Desert Herb Farm – bloomindesertherbs.com
- Young Living – Therapeutic Grade Essential Oils , Quality

personal care products and Diffusers – YoungLiving.com
*Note: if you already work with a Young Living Distributor, please honor that relationship for ordering. If you are not currently working with a distributor or you are interested in becoming one, please see my website or see Resources in the back of the book.

NOTES:

Habit 70

Post-Travel Habits

What:

When you return it is important to establish some beneficial habits when you come home. These habits range in purpose from suitcase care to connection time with family all the way to parasite cleansing. How about that for a span of habit topics?

Why:

Traveling carries with it many challenges both on the road and once home. Check out habits #64 Hotel Hygiene and #71 Don't Bring Home Hitchhikers which are designed to keep you as well as your family safe and healthy. I'm guessing that NOT bringing bed bugs, athlete's foot and other fun fungi and parasites home to your family is pretty high on their lists for Post-Travel Habits.

Also check out #72 Building in a Recovery Day and #75 Investing in Peaceful Returns as ways to reconnect with your spouse, children or circle of friends. Reconnection deserves debriefing from both sides – the travelers and the ones holding down the fort at home. This keeps all parties informed of both mountain top experiences as well as the fun or challenging times. Making this time a priority is vital for feeling a sense of sharing life with each other.

How To:

- For those at home, stop what you are doing if possible, get up and go greet the traveler.
- For longer trips, it's always nice to have a special greeting for the weary traveler as well as the weary adult holding the fort down at home.
- Unload and unpack as soon as possible especially if you travel frequently. That suitcase by the front door can get old greeting everyone when they walk in.
- After you empty your suitcase, spray with a non toxic sanitizer and let it air out.
- Make time for everyone in the household to share experiences.
- It is a good idea to do a parasite cleanse at least once a year, if you travel outside your home country, perhaps twice a year. A good parasite cleanse will have a routine of three weeks on, one week off and repeat cycle three times.
- Get laundry going right away if another trip is coming soon. It's easy to forget.
- Go for a walk or get to an exercise class or gym.
- Take an Epsom Salt Detox bath.

Related Healthy Habits:
- #22 Epsom Salt Soak
- #43 The Cleanse
- #71 Don't Bring Home Hitchhikers
- #72 Building in a Recovery Day
- #75 Investing in Peaceful Returns

Resources:

- Parasite Cleansing – Parafree Capsules – youngliving.org
- Theives Spray or Theives Household Cleaner – Young Living – Therapeutic Grade Essential Oils , Quality personal care products and Diffusers – YoungLiving.com *Note: if you already work with a Young Living Distributor, please honor that relationship for ordering. If you are not currently working with a distributor or you are interested in becoming one, please see my website or see Resources in the back of the book.

Don't Bring Home
Hitchhikers

What:

Just say no. There really is no "fun" fungi, so please don't bring any back to your household.

Why:

For some years now we have heard about a resurgence of bed bugs. YUK! They can and do bite and are hard to get rid of once they have established themselves in your home.

How To:

- In the hotel: Bring a small glass spray bottle with colloidal silver, water or vinegar mixed with about 10 drops of Purification Blend essential Oil. Spray the dresser drawers before putting clothes in them with this mixture.
- Upon Return: Empty suitcases and spray them with same mixture or with Thieves spray or a mixture of the Thieves Household Cleaner or white distilled vinegar.
  - It is important to cleanse your body upon return.

- Vacuum out your dresser drawers monthly, wash clothes upon your return and spray suitcases.

Related Healthy Habits:
- #43 The Cleanse
- #70 Post Travel Habits/Cleanse

Resources:
- Thieves Household Cleaner/Thieves Spray/Purification Essential oil Blend – young living.org
- White Distilled Vinegar is available at most grocery stores.
- Glass Spray Bottles (many sizes) – abundanthealth4u.com

Build in Recovery Day

What:

Building in a Recovery Day is important for when you have been away either for long periods, long distances or for intense reasons. Purposefully do not schedule anything if at all possible so that your body can readjust to the time zone and normal routines and support your spouse who has been holding down the fort.

Why:

Your Body, Mind and Soul needs to reset itself after large journeys. Perhaps your loved ones need time to readjust to you after a major life experience or simply arduous journey.

How To:

- Keep your calendar empty or light the first day back.
- Hire a babysitter and have a date night with your spouse.
- Sleep.
- Drink plenty of fluids. Many people become dehydrated while traveling and don't even realize it. Hydrate!

Related Healthy Habits:

- #31 Eat, Sleep, Drink – Ms. Mary's Mantra
- #67 Being Present While Away
- #75 Invest in Your Peaceful Return

Resources:

- No Resources – Just simply be!

Habit 73

Vary Vacation's Vocation

What:

Practice going on different types of getaways by varying the Vacation's Vocation

1. Rest & Rejuvenation
2. Creative & Inspiration
3. Action & Adventure

Thank you to Kim and Jim Thomas of Say-So for sharing this habit with me.

Why:

Because some periods in your life require time to simply rest, while others are more about rejuvenation of creativity and inspiration. Once rejuvenated, the action and adventure vacations can really revitalize our whole being. The action and adventure can be big like mountain climbing or personally significant like facing a fear or trying something totally out of our comfort zones.

How To:

- First and most importantly, block off the times for vacation.
- If married, take at least one getaway as a couple without the

kiddos – Wise Investment.

- Start folders, scrapbooks or Pinterest pages for ideas for these different types of getaways
- Protect these vacations as if it means your life ...because they do!
- Consider staycations. These are cheaper and easier to pull off, but keep them sacred and don't be tempted to go off course and get back to regular life.
- Keep a special savings account for vacations
- Think of vacations as an longterm investment with HUGE payoff.

Related Healthy Habits:
- #74 Book Your Next Vacation Soon

Resources:
- **The Artist's Way** by Julia Cameron
- Your Strategic Attraction Plan (SAP)
- **Chi-To-Be** book, audio recordings and coaching by Stacey Hall – chi-to-be.com (SAP)
- **Attracting the Perfect Customer** by Stacey Hall and Jan Brogniez (SAP)
- Kim and Jim Thomas – Say-So a great Christian duo and all around awesome couple
- The Village Chapel – Nashville, TN – thevillagechapel.com

Habit 74

Book Your Next Vacation Soon

What:

Book your vacation or at least block out the time period that you will go on vacation soon. Many people wait too long to plan their vacations and have a difficult time finding a time period that works for the whole family. Many people who travel for a living don't think of going somewhere else again as vacation; they'd rather have a stay-cation. However, their families are usually the ones at home and would love a getaway. Vacation time with family is great and best if not mixed with business unless that has been defined before.

For example, every year Mike gets to participate in a Youth Citizenship Seminar (YCS) at Pepperdine University in Malibu. The family gets to come but knows beforehand that he has certain obligations while we are there. We get to hear great speakers, hang with fabulous young adults, the kids get to join their dad on stage and we all get beach time. A free vacation and everybody wins!

Why:

If you don't book it or block off the time, something else will come along and fill that space and then you realize that it's been five years since your last vacation. Exhaustion, overwhelm, boredom do not contribute to our well being. Vacations break the monotony, can put the spark back into our hearts and spring back into our step.

How To:

- Keep alert for getaways that speak to you.
- Ask friends about trips they have taken as a family.
- Write vacation ideas down and decide together.

Related Healthy Habits:

- #29 Release, Rest and Rejuvenate
- #74 Vary Vacation's Vocation

Resources:

- Watch the travel channel for a few nights in a row to spark ideas for destinations.
- Block off travel periods on your calendar immediately.

Habit 75

Invest in Your Peaceful Return

What:

Invest in a peaceful return home rather than being hurried or having to jump right into catch up mode. Whether you are single, married, with kids or not, having a little white space when you walk in the door rather than hitting the ground running helps adjusting back into life and allow your trip to sink in well.

This habit applies even if everyone was along for the trip. The goal is walking in the door again refreshed and happy to be home. The tone of the family arriving back home can create anchors with vacation time. If everyone has a good attitude and helps unpack the car or bring in suitcases, it can be a positive anchor with travel.

Why:

Whether your trip was business or pleasure, it is really tough to return only to immediately start spinning a bunch of plates. If you were traveling by yourself and returning home to loved ones, it's really important to make sure you can be home and present for them. That may mean saying hello and taking a quick nap so you are refreshed for a special movie night together or spending some time sharing the day's events. The idea is to create positive anchors with travel and vacations. When there is an uplifting association with coming home, there is fertile ground for connection for everyone.

How To:

- If everyone has been gone, hire someone to clean the house before you get back. It is much better to return to than piles of laundry and mess from the day you left.
- Keep your calendar empty or light the first day back.
- If you've been away, hire a babysitter and have a date night with your spouse.
- Plan one-on-one time with each of your children.
- Ask your family if there is anything special they would like to do together.
- If you had a physically or emotionally challenging trip, then schedule a massage for you and for your spouse who stayed home.
- Allow for Release, Rest and Rejuvenation.
- Leave white space to allow your journey's experience to fully realize. Journaling is great for this.

Related Healthy Habits:
- #22 Epsom Soaks #66 Invest in Massage, Steams and Saunas #67 Being Present While Away

Resources:

- To find a local Spa – spafinder.com
- Release, Rest and Rejuvenate post on The Healthy Habit Coach blog – thehealthyhabitcoach.com/health-and-wellness/release-rest-rejuvenation

"Don't spend your precious time asking
"Why isn't the world a better place?"
It will only be time wasted.
The question to ask is
"How can I make it better?"
To that there is an answer."

– Dr. Leo Buscaglia

Healthy Habits for Community

Introduction

I once received great advice from an Ayurvdic Doctor and former neighbor of mine, Dr. Sudir Kapila. He spoke straight into my soul "Start at home. Start in your neighborhood and in your community. Start at home." He was referring to teaching, sharing, uplifting others with health and support, and starting with myself and my family first. He was so right. Starting with one's self, family and immediate community is very important in the worldwide online community access we now have. The beauty is that we can now share what we are doing at home simultaneously with others throughout the world. I love sharing recipes, successes and blunders with my blog followers as far away as Russia, Malaysia and Australia, but I know that first, I still must "start at home".

I have been blessed with getting to know many health bloggers and advocates around the globe. I have also been blessed with ways to share my family's challenges and successes with a global community. When you share health via blogs, presentations, coaching, books, etc. it can be easy to get so immersed in coaching others that you can let your own health or your family's health slide for the sake of the world. One can become so focused on getting the next book or post up, that they forget about a grieving neighbor and how much they might appreciate a meal being prepared for them. In my experience, these efforts go hand in hand. We each have our journeys and can be practicing and sharing healthy habits alongside each other.

I also know many great souls on the opposite side of this coin. They are so immersed and overwhelmed taking care of ill loved ones or managing chronic illness themselves, that they can't even seem to take time to learn and practice some new healthy habits to uplift their lives. My heart goes out to those in this place. I do what I do to reverse this trend of needless illness in our world. If we can each create better health for ourselves and then share habit #76 Teach Them to Fish we can perhaps reverse the current trend of poor habits and poor health in our world.

The Healthy Habits for Community section is devoted to showing you how to create healthy ripples in your home and in your community. The goal is to be sustainable and practice habit #92 Off Balance on Purpose (Dan Thurmon). Yes, we have our virtual communities and that can be fabulous. It is equally as important, if not more so, to turn our attention to our own habits and the health of the people actually present in our lives. Caring for our physically present community is vital to the health of our world. Caring for our own health is a tremendous investment in the quality of life for us all. The beauty is that these lessons learned through blood, sweat and tears can then be shared with the world now with a click of a button. Please create and share your own Healthy Habits for Community. Be the ripple!

Habit 76

Teach Them To Fish

What:

"Give a man a fish and you feed him for a day. Teach a man to fish and you feed him for a lifetime." – phrase was coined by Anne Isabella Thackeray Ritchie (1837–1919) in her novel, Mrs. Dymond (1885)

I love the wisdom of this old adage. It took many years for me to learn its wisdom, and I seem to need to re-learn it often. I can support many more people by inspiring them to create and practice uplifting habits themselves than by trying to do it for them. I also have come to realize that they have to want to be healthy more than I want them to be.

Why:

It is a great gift to bring someone a meal, but you can feed them much longer when you teach them to cook the meal. If you can inspire others and teach them healthy habits to add to their lives, maybe they will stay well and be able to teach others. All too often well meaning people bring a box of chocolates to someone who is ill. I have never witnessed so many chronically ill people as in this generation. I believe we can reverse this trend if we support each other by sharing healthy habits and practicing ways to #2

Manage our Buckets better. Instead of chocolates, how about bringing over a funny movie or cooking lunch for them while you explain what you are making. (Hint: make it simple and fun to create a positive anchor for them.)

Another side to this habit is that there are many givers in our world who will literally make themselves sick trying to keep up with doing for others. Don't get me wrong, serving is in my opinion one of the greatest acts we can do for others and is truly what we are each called to be doing. I am talking specifically to those who serve and give so much that their own health falters. We live in a fallen world with people with needs far greater than any of us can constantly fill. It is vital to support others in a way that doesn't enable them but "teaches them to fish" so they can feel better and teach others how to fish. Hence, "Be the Ripple."

I remember bringing chicken broth to my friend Christine who was very ill with multiple layers of issues. Her doctor was getting ready to put her in the hospital, and she pleaded for a few more days to turn things around. I brought over chicken broth. Good old fashioned, 24 hour simmered chicken broth. Her body soaked it up. She went through it quickly. I knew I couldn't keep pace making it as fast as she could go through it. I realized that she was getting her energy back, so the following week, I brought over all the ingredients and we made broth together in her own home. It's not hard to make; it just takes 24 hours to simmer in order to get all of the nutrients out of the bones. We had fun together and laughed throughout the process. This created positive anchors for her with both cooking and eating nutrient rich food.

When her husband came home and smelled the broth cooking,

it reminded him of his mother's cooking when he was a boy. This positive anchor with the smell of chicken broth simmering seemed to spark something in him too. Between his positive anchor and his own health challenges, his body soaked up the broth as well. This one habit learned and applied changed the course of their health issues. It energized their bodies and their minds, which gave them the ability to continue learning and applying more healthy habits and healing many other areas of their lives.

How To:

Giving is nice and necessary sometimes and hopefully encourages "Pay it Forward" mentality. Teaching is an investment of time that pays off exponentially. Share and teach healthy habits to your spouse, your children, your family and friends. You may have big arms and a great heart, but you simply cannot do everything for everyone. When you teach and inspire others to add healthy habits, your efforts are exponential and affect many more lives than if you stick to always giving. Make sense?

Related Healthy Habits:
*   #1-100
*   #77 Share Healthy Habits

Resources:

*   Your own hard earned lessons and habits can be a gold mine for other people to start on the path to wellness and wholeness.
*   Teach Them to Fish Foundation – teachthemtofish.org (I do not know them personally, but they sound like my kind of group.)
*   **100 Easy Healthy Habits** audio coaching series and book by Tara Rayburn

Habit 77

Share Healthy Habits - Be the Ripple!

What:

In Healthy Habit #76 Teach Them to Fish, we talk about how important teaching healthy habits can be for you, your family and your community. Sharing and teaching traditional healthy habits used to be common in our world. These life lessons were passed down from generation to generation. Some healthy traditions are cross-cultural, like eating digestible food and getting probiotics through cultured foods and beverages. Other habits can be specific to genetics, heritage, race and religion. For example, following Kosher or Amish traditions isn't simply a dietary preference; for many it is part of their faith and heritage. Generations of practicing certain habits can imprint in families for the better or the worse.

Today we have lost much of that teaching and sharing with families living very far away from each other, as well as many people have caved in to the "fast-food, fast-track lifestyle." Now thanks to the internet and resources like The Weston A.

Price Foundation, we can be learning and sharing these habits, recipes, tips and principles for health at a local level as well as a worldwide capacity.

Why:

You can support many more lives by teaching and sharing information with others than by repetitively "doing" for them. Inspiring, sharing and learning from each other creates strong relationships and good health. Strong relationships and good health create a strong healthy community. Stronger and healthier communities create a better world to live in. Being the Ripple is an amazing way to uplift our world.

How To:

- Start a cooking class or healthy habits group.
- Find and join a local Weston Price Chapter to find resources (books, DVD's, attend and promote events).
- Go to your local community center and see what they offer or find out what it takes to teach a class or lead a group.
- Attend a Wise Traditions, Body Ecology or Young Living Convention.
- Start listening to or participating in a variety of health oriented webinars.
- Write a book, blog or article in the local paper.
- Vow to add one healthy habit a month.
- When people express curiosity about what you are doing or why you seem so healthy, be willing to share simple, sound habits with them.
- Purchase "Nourishing Our Children" and teach the class in your community.
- Encourage and inspire others.

Related Healthy Habits:

- #1- 100 #40 Encourage
- #75 Teach Them to Fish
- #82 Host a Soup Swap

Resources:

- **100 Easy Healthy Habits** audio series and book by Tara Rayburn
- Wise Traditions Convention/Weston A. Price Foundation – westonapricefoundation.org
- Price-Pottenger Nutrition Foundation – ppnf.org
- Chef Monica Corrado – Cooking Classes, Educational Materials, Training – simplybeingwell.com
- Check into your local community centers for classes (to take or to teach).
- Nourishing Our Children nourishingourchildren.org

Make a Pot-o-Soup

What:

Make a huge pot of homemade soup and can, freeze or just seal tightly in glass canning jars -it lasts a very long time in the fridge.

Why:

Whether you just keep broth on hand, pull soup out of the freezer or canning jars, soup is the ultimate fast food. Soup is nutrient rich fast food and is easily absorbed and assimilated for supporting health and wellness. It is also a great community builder (see #82 Host a Soup Swap).

How To:

First, make a huge pot of broth (see #7 **Stock with Stocks**) and can, freeze or simply roll right into soup. Next, find or create one or two basic soup recipes. Remember to #30 **Engage the Whole Family** by helping wash, peel and chop. Either learn to can or freeze your soups. If you know that you are going to have a busy day, pull a jar of soup out from the freezer the night before to thaw. You can also use your homemade stock or buy organic stock from a local farm or health food store. Just add leftovers, fresh herbs and veggies and in less than 20 minutes you'll have an amazing dinner!

> **NOTE:** When you freeze in glass canning jars, you must leave at least two inches of breathing space and let the soup completely cool before freezing. It is still challenging not to have the glass break in the freezer. The most stable method is freezing in glass Pyrex with tight lids, but allow for complete cooling before placing in freezer.

Related Healthy Habits:
- #82 Host A Soup Swap
- #86 Community Unity Potlucks

Resources:
- **Essential Gluten-Free Recipes 2nd Edition** by Tara Rayburn and Mary Vars
- **Overcoming Cancer: A Journey of Faith** by Judi Moreo – judimoreo.com
- The Healthy Habit Coach website for "How To" videos and recipes – theHealthyHabitCoach.com
- **Nourishing Traditions** by Sally Fallon Morell and Mary Enig
- Chef Monica Corrado – Cooking Classes, Educational Materials, Training – simplybeingwell.com
- Chef Shane Kelly – Real Food Real Healing – chefshanekelly.com
- **Nourishing Broth** by Sally Fallon Morrell and Kaayla Daniel – Coming in 2014! Nourishing Broth via Grand Central Publishing

Habit 79

Natural Breath Fresheners

New York Times health columnist Jane E. Brody has written that she receives more questions about bad breath than about any other common medical problem.

What:

Chronic bad breath, or halitosis, is a huge deterrent for communication and connection with others. Talk about a community crasher. Whether you are the offender or the offended, it makes it difficult to focus and be really present and attentive while interacting. Addressing the problem at the root cause is the most effective way to eradicate it.

Why:

Causes for halitosis can range from plaque buildup to food stuck in between teeth, undiagnosed cavities, lung or sinus infections to major diseases and systemic fungal infection (yeast overgrowth is oftentimes referred to as Candida overgrowth).

How To:

Obviously addressing the balance of body flora in your body is key for not just breath but overall body odor too. My dentist actually takes a sample of my saliva and shows the video of what is present. YUK! Adding probiotics to your daily diet can not only help with breath but body odor too. Destroying funky fungi and other pathogens involves dietary changes. Lose the sugars and empty starches and practice healthy germ killing dental habits.

Daily Dental Habits for Beating Beastly Breath:
Brush Teeth with Non Toxic Toothpaste: Don't let your toothpaste be another vehicle for adding toxins to your body. Do your homework. Fluoride is not the miracle it was once proposed to be. There are many wonderful herbs and toothpastes available that don't need toxins to keep your mouth fresh.

Flossing and Specialized Toothpick Brushes: Flossing is perhaps the most important tool for your pearly whites and for having healthy gums. The new brush/toothpicks are great for cleaning and stimulating the gums, but be sure they are not too rough and damage your gums. I keep both of these tools in my purse now. As I have gotten older the chances of food getting stuck or accumulation between my teeth has increased. In fact, about five years ago I had four areas that food painfully accumulated after every meal. YUK and OW! By using consistent healthy Dental Habits, I have reduced this to only one area that occasionally causes issues.

Coconut Oil Pulling: After brushing and flossing, swish vigorously with coconut oil for 10-20 minutes, spit into a toilet and flush immediately. Spitting into a sink is a germ fest and clogged pipe waiting to happen. Then brush again, swish and gargle with Thieves mouthwash or another NON-Toxic mouthwash. Coconut oil is VERY antimicrobial and draws bacteria out of the gums and from in between the teeth. If there is a chronic issue I may add a drop of clove, Thieves or oregano essential oil to the mix as an extra anti-microbial element. Be sure to brush and gargle well after in order to avoid any potential corrosive effects.

Peppermint or Thieves Essential Oil: Take a food grade anti-microbial essential oil and either dilute or put a tiny amount and run into gums directly. VERY STRONG – try dilution first. You can also put one drop on your finger and run a little into the inside of your cheek to avoid overloading your tastebuds. Warning: Water and Essential Oils do not mix. Water will amplify the sensation. Best to start with less and work your way to more and have olive or coconut oil handy for dilution.

Related Healthy Habits:
- #4 Be Probiotic
- #9 Eat REAL Food

Resources:
- Peppermint Essential Oil and Thieves Mouthwash – abundanceandwisdom.com/tararayburn
- **Cure Tooth Decay** by Ramiel Nagel – curetoothdecay.com
- Spry Gum and Breath Mints sweetened with Xylitol from Vitacost.com
- Coconut Oil Pulling and Research – coconutresearchcenter.org
- Coconut Oil – tropicaltraditions.com or greenpasture.org or spectrumorganics.com

- Bell Center for Holistic Dentistry – Dr. Michael Bell – lvtmjdentist.com
- **Body Ecology** by Donna Gates – bodyecology.com

NOTES:

Habit 80

Presentation is Key

What:

How it looks can make or break the "love it or hate it" factor. Presentation isn't everything, but it does create the first impression. An attractive presentation is the first factor in the decision to like or even try a food or beverage. I cannot tell you how many interesting foods and beverages I've gotten my kids and their friends to try by using brightly colored ceramic bowls or glasses. For that matter, the same is true for the adults.

Why:

Pleasing the eye is the best bribery for the taste buds. Although, sometimes bribery works well too ;-) Once there has been enough history of good tastes following pleasant presentations, you might be able to try some items that don't always look nice. That's where straight up bribery comes in handy.

I bribed my kids one time to take just one bite of grass fed beef liver. I figured worst case scenario would be that I'd be out two dollars and they would hate liver. Fifteen dollars later my son asked me if he could do it again the next day so he could buy light sabers for both he and his sister. Although I don't bribe with money anymore, we still laugh about that story, and my son has a positive association with liver. It certainly didn't hurt that I served the liver on my Granny Pearl's china with wonderful style and fabulous presentation.

How To:

- Look for sales on fun shaped Le Crueset or glass bowls and cups. They can really be inexpensive and dress up a dish nicely. NO Plastic Please #13 Water Wisdom.
- Grow or purchase organic herbs, edible flowers, veggies or fruit to dress up presentations.
- Decorate the table or eating area with fresh flowers, naturally scented candles or placemats.
- Watch food channels or visit blogs, Pinterest boards etc for ideas.
- Keep a camera nearby to post photos so you can help inspire others.

Related Healthy Habits:

- #46 Create Healthy Traditions

Resources:

- **Essential Gluten-Free Recipes 2nd Edition** by Tara Rayburn and Mary Vars
- Mary Vars, Mentor Mom and Masterful Artist of the Aesthetic Presentation of Food :-D
- Chef Monica Corrado – SimplyWell.com
- Chef Shane Kelley – Real Food Real Healing – chefshanekelly. com
- For Ideas go to Pinterest – pinterest.com/tararayburn or

Instagram -instagram.com/healthyhabits.

- Bloomin Desert Herbs – bloomindesertherbs.com
- Le Crueset – cookware – lecreuset.com

NOTES:

Accountability
Responsibility

What:

Ultimately you are accountable to yourself and to God. Period.

Why:

When you know who you are and what you stand for, you also know what you are holding yourself accountable for. Some people do like having external tangible accountability partners and join weight loss or exercise groups. This is fine as long as there are some established guidelines like "no guilt" and "no shaming" etc.

How To:

- Know what you are accountable to yourself and to your Maker for. Are you someone who keeps your word? Are you someone who does not lie or cheat? Are you a person determined to be a better version of yourself daily? You get the idea.
- If you join a group or hire a coach, have clear rules and practices. Fear and shame are not positive anchors for adding healthy habits and keeping accountability.

Related Healthy Habits:

- #2 Manage Your Bucket
- #21 Exercise as a Habit
- #41 Be True to Your Quest

Resources:

- Stacy Hall *Chi-To-Be: Achieving Your Ultimate B-All Accountability and SAP – www.chi-to-be.com
- Healthy Habits Meetup Group – meetup.com/HealthyHabitsLasVegas

Habit 82

Host a Soup Swap

What:

A Soup Swap is a gathering where participants each bring a crock pot or stock pot of soup, its recipe and extra quart size glass canning jars to swap samples. You can share these recipes by printing out copies, e-mailing them, or posting them online with photos so you can share with more of your community.

Why:

A Soup Swap is a great community builder because it's fun trying other people's recipes, creating relationships and positive associations with eating REAL, Nourishing food.

TIP: Find out in advance if there is anyone in the community recovering from surgery or suffering from chronic health issues and you can collect soup jars to bring to them after the event. You talk about creating smiles and community – Wow!

How To:

- Have people bring a crock pot or stockpot of soup along

with its recipe, mugs for taste testing other soups and extra canning jars to swap soups or collect for someone in need.

- Invite individuals or post at your church, community center, school or join and collaborate with a local farm and/or Weston A. Price Foundation Chapter.
- Join, Create or Post on a group message board online like through Meetup.com.

Related Healthy Habits:
- #76 Teach Them To Fish
- #77 Share Healthy Habits
- #86 Community Unity Potlucks

Resources:
- Weston A. Price Foundation Chapter Leaders – westonaprice. org/local-chapters/find-local-chapter
- **Overcoming Cancer: A Journey of Faith** by Judi Moreo – judimoreo.com
- **Nourishing Traditions** by Sally Fallon Morell and Mary Enig for Soup and Broth Recipes
- Meetup.com for local groups interested in health, community, food, healthy play groups, etc.
- Glass Quart Size Canning Jars – jarstore.com

Habit 83

Change a Habit, Change a Life

What:

Decide right now to change or add an uplifting habit for the Mind, Body and Soul.

Why:

If we are not being proactive with our health and finding ways to nourish and cleanse daily with REAL food and un-suppressive measures, we are setting ourselves and our families up for health issues.

How To:

- Adding a habit is usually easier psychologically than quitting a habit.
- Start small and commit to one week.
- After one week, review, keep or choose a new one, repeat process.

Related Healthy Habits:

- #1 – Simply Start
- #1-100 Pick one and go!

Resources:

- **100 Easy Healthy Habits** Audio and Book by Tara Rayburn – thehealthyhabitcoach.com/books
- The Healthy Habit Coach Blog – thehealthyhabitcoach.com/blog
- Dr. Joseph Mercola Website – Mercola.com
- Dr. Kaayla Daniel – drkaayladaniel.com
- Village Green Network Bloggers – villagegreennetwork.com

Make Your Own Personal Care Products - Together

What:

Give or take a class on how to create your own personal care products. It is important to use a reliable resource or existing recipe as there may be skin sensitivity, allergic reactions or major detox effects…Just ask me about the avocado and lime mask my daughter made :-)

Why:

Our bodies are completely bombarded daily by toxins. Most of the offenders enter our bodies via personal care products like shampoo, soaps, makeup, deodorant and many more synthetically created and chemically odorized toiletries.

How To:

- Take, give or host a "How To…" class.
- Use a book or very reliable resource.
- Find out if anyone has allergies or skin sensitivities before putting anything in-on-or around the participants.

- Always test on a small portion of skin first.
- Have a Spa Themed Birthday Party or Ladies Night out.

Related Healthy Habits:
- #18 Personal Care Purification

Resources:

- Environmental Working Group – EWG.org
- **Bamboo Jade Soaps and Candles** by Debbie Alcazar, Japan – bamboo-jade.com
- **Earthly Bodies and Heavenly Hair: Natural & Healthy Body Care For Everybody** by Dina Falconi
- **Beauty By God** by Shelley Ballestero - shellyballestero.com
- My Beautiful Truth – mybeautifultruth.com
- Young Living – Therapeutic Grade Essential Oils , Quality personal care products and Diffusers – YoungLiving.com *Note: if you already work with a Young Living Distributor, please honor that relationship for ordering. If you are not currently working with a distributor or you are interested in becoming one, please see my website or see Resources in the back of the book.

Host a Movie Showing

What:

Host a showing of a health related movie in your home or a local venue with the intention of creating awareness, dialogue and community improvement.

Why:

Ignorance is not bliss. When people understand more about what is affecting their health, they can make better decisions and vote with their dollar.

How To:

- You can host a showing in your home, your church, local community center or doctor's office.
- You can collaborate with local farmers, farmer's markets, holistic wellness professionals and rent a bigger venue like a vintage movie theater or movie in the park.
- If the topic is long and/or heavy, I encourage you to hold a town center type meeting or have a panel discussion to help people process and feel empowered.

Related Healthy Habits:

- #1-100 Any of these topics would be great subject matter for a movie showing.

Resources:

- For Movies and Resources – Weston A. Price Foundation Chapter Leader Locator – westonaprice.org/local-chapters/find-local-chapter
- **Genetic Roulette** book and documentary by Jeffery Smith – geneticroulettemovie.com
- The NON-GMO Project – nongmoproject.org
- Two Angry Moms – angrymoms.org
- Wise Tradition Conference DVD's and CD's – fleetwoodonsite.com

Habit 86

Community Unity
Potlucks

What:

Have a periodic potluck (monthly, quarterly, annually) with the intention of sharing nourishing foods and beverages together and building community. This is even more powerful if you can collaborate with a local farm and have it onsite. Some farms host what is called a Farm to Fork dinner or a breakfast for shareholders.

Why:

Something amazing happens when you "break bread" together. There is a wonderful intangible that speaks to your soul – if you are eating REAL food that is. Otherwise, it can become a bloat-fest of epic gluttony proportions.

How To:

- Just start by having a potluck dinner.
- Be sure to give any parameters and considerations if there are specific allergy or dietary necessities. For example, you

can request everyone include an ingredient list or "no nuts" or request items with certain ingredients be labeled as such. "Contains: Dairy"

- Contact a local organic farm and see if they might be interested in hosting a potluck on premises.

Related Healthy Habits:
- #2 Share Healthy Habits
- #82 Host a Soup Swap

Resources:

- Weston A. Price Foundation Chapter Leader Locator – westonaprice.org/local-chapters/find-local-chapter
- Find Local Farmer's Markets – localharvest.org
- Two Great Farms building community on their farms:
    - Quail Hollow Farm in Overton, NV – quailhollowfarmcsa.com
    - Fields of Athenry in Purcellville, VA – fieldsofathenryfarm.com
- Search Online for local Community Centers or ask a local church about collaboration

Keep Health Within Reach

What:

Keeping your Health Within Reach has a few meanings. First, it is keeping healthy foods and beverages physically handy and convenient for grab and go lifestyle. Next, Keeping Health Within Reach means setting realistic goals especially when you are just beginning to create uplifting habits. Finally, I think of this habit as sharing realistic uplifting habits with others in a simple, doable way. K-I-S-S (keep it simple sweetie).

Why:

Grab and Go: We all have busy schedules, we tend to grab what we can see and carry easily. Most of the time these aren't very digestible choices. Keep healthy options on the counter with necessary bags, bowls or glasses. Good grab and go choices can uplift your health more than you will ever know.

Realistic Goal-Setting: See #1 Simply Start with a very easy way to set your health goals. Generally, it is best to set yourself up for success by adding a habit instead of quitting one.

How To:

- Start with a simple and easy to accomplish habit to get the ball rolling in the right direction.
- Keep healthy snacks conveniently located for grab and go availability.

Check out these recipes for handy nutrient rich snacks from Essential Gluten Free Recipes:

- Counter Top Convenience (p.165)
- Essential Oil Infused Date Ball (p. 171)
- Beef Jerky w/ Essential Oils (p. 179)
- Essential Fruit Leathers (p. 185)

Related Healthy Habits:

- #1 Start Simply – Simply Start
- #9 Eat Real Food

Resources:

- **Essential Gluten-Free Recipes 2nd Edition** by Tara Rayburn and Mary Vars – lifesciencepublishers.com
- Mary Vars, Mentor Mom and Masterful Artist of the Aesthetic Presentation of Food :-D
- Chef Monica Corrado – SimplyWell.com
- Chef Shane Kelley – Real Food Real Healing – chefshanekelly.com

Habit 88

Be Aromatic

What:

Allow your aroma to benefit your health, as well as those around you with natural uplifting aromas. Your aroma can actually create a positive anchor/association for others with uplifting habits for their own health and wellbeing. Essential oils, herbs and products using natural, organic ingredients are uplifting and have amazing aromas supportive to your health that can help your body detox instead of adding to your toxic load.

Another area to consider in being Aromatic is your home or office. Do you keep synthetically made candles, soaps and potpourri throughout your house? These "Odorizers" simply mask smells by pouring synthetic chemicals into your system. Once you have been away from synthetic smells for awhile, you can tell a difference. There are plenty of sources to buy or make your own candles, soaps and potpourri from essential oils so you can purify the air and your home rather than "toxify" it. Cool Mist Essential Oils Diffusers are fantastic for sanitizing the air quality in your home, as well as you end up carrying the aroma along with you on your clothing and hair. Nice Perk ;-)

Why:

Most perfumes, colognes and scented body products have been created synthetically in a lab. Cost doesn't equal quality. Some of the most expensive perfumes are toxins in a pretty bottle. Man cannot duplicate in a lab what mother nature or more importantly God can create in nature. Sometimes natural ingredients are used but then altered and added to products claiming to be "natural." However, once these elements are changed, they no longer have the symbiotic uplifting balance to be a supportive force and can actually create health issues.

Synthetic ingredients can add to the toxic load in your body compromising your health and the health of those around you. Today there are more chemically sensitive people and allergic reactions to these synthetic chemicals than ever before. I know my daughter's school doesn't allow scented products in the locker room because of possible allergic reactions.

How To:

- I use therapeutic grade essential oils for my "perfume." I usually carry an essential oil pouch in my purse with roll ons (already diluted with coconut oil) and a variety of oils which range in purpose from basic wonderfully aromatic purposes like Joy Blend, to specific health supporting oils like peppermint for digestion and breath freshening.
- Make your own potpourri: Add two to eight drops of your favorite essential oils to a beautiful bowl of pine cones, sea shells or other non synthetically scented items. If you can, close them up in a glass jar for a few hours to become deeply infused and then display them in your home.
- For basic body detox and moisturizing see #24 Oilination.

- Cool Mist Diffusing is an amazing way to sanitize the air in your home while uplifting your family's health at the same time.

Related Healthy Habits:
- #18 Personal Care Product Purification
- #24 Oilination
- #55 Essential Oil Checklist
- #84 Make Your Own Skin Care Products

Resources:

- Environmental Working Group – EWG.org
- **Bamboo Jade Essential Oil Soaps and Candles** by Debbie Alcazar, Japan – bamboo-jade.com
- **Earthly Bodies and Heavenly Hair: Natural & Healthy Body Care For Everybody** by Dina Falconi
- **Beauty By God** by Shelley Ballestero
- Young Living – Therapeutic Grade Essential Oils , Quality personal care products and Diffusers – YoungLiving.com *Note: if you already work with a Young Living Distributor, please honor that relationship for ordering. If you are not currently working with a distributor or you are interested in becoming one, please see my website or see Resources in the back of the book.
- Cool Mist Diffuser – purchase via the link on my blog and receive a discount – thehealthyhabitcoach.com/blog or go to DiffuserWorld.com and use coupon code – A735SAVE5
- **Essential Oils Desk Reference** or **Pocket Guide** from Life Science Publishing – lifesciencepublishers.com

Habit 89

What to Do When You Don't Know What to Do

What:

Have you ever found yourself around a crisis situation and had no idea how to help or felt like there really wasn't much you could do? This is the perfect time to get simple. In the most basic form, sometimes just "holding space" with someone is the most precious gift you can give. Other times it can be holding a hand, massaging feet or bringing a funny movie over to watch. Listening with the intention of understanding and not replying is a skill and a gift. All of these things are the simple acts of sharing your time and focused attention on another human being. These practices are very valuable gifts in these busy times.

Why:

Appropriate touch is a basic human need. Many people are starved of this need. Being heard and understood is priceless. Just having someone silently present is sometimes the best gift possible. Many people are living alone and unheard.

While living in Las Vegas, I have never heard so many people in such a populated area complain of loneliness, lack of friends and sense of community.

How To:

- Practice the art of #29 Release, Rest and Rejuvenation
- Wake well and become grounded. Rest can open the mind to new ideas and solutions.
- Read 30 Ways to Help in Helpless Situations by Rob Payne
- Follow Everyday is Precious blog by Rob Payne

Related Healthy Habits:

- #27 Waking Well
- #29 Release, Rest and Rejuvenate

Resources:

- The Healthy Habit Coach Blog – thehealthyhabitcoach.com/blog
- **30 Ways to Help in Helpless Situations** by Rob Payne
- "Every Day is Precious" – robscolumns.wordpress.com
- Blessing Ranch/Blessing Bay – Dr. John Walker, Dr. Charity Walker and Deanna Walker – blessingranch.org
- Verve Online Broadcasts – live.mediasocial.tv/verve
- Verve Archived Broadcasts – vimeo.com/channels/watchverve

Habit 90

Have an Attitude of
Gratitude

"It's not what happens in life, it's what you do about it."

– W. Mitchell

What:

I've actually heard this quote by several people and each one of them has a special story why they are so uniquely qualified to share this message. We are each qualified to practice its wisdom. We all experience pain, joy, grief, happiness, sorrow, anger…you name it. It is easy to feel sorry for ourselves sometimes or feel that nobody could possibly understand our situation. The truth is: character is usually developed through experiencing hardship and coming out the other side.

Why:

Many people end up hanging their hat on their hardship. They actually settle into what I call victim mentality. The problem is that this will only get you more of the same – situations that allow you to repeatedly play the victim. When you decide to stop focusing on being a victim and start focusing on who you choose to be, your life will transform.

How To:

- Start your day with the first thought being something like this: "Thank you, God, for this day and all its lessons, blessings and people. Please allow me to use it all to your good use."
- Choose to experience the blessing in every situation, no matter how long it takes to realize.

Related Healthy Habits:
- #27 Waking Well
- #40 Encourage
- #48 Focus on the Shoot
- #92 Live Off Balance on Purpose
- #94 See What Isn't There
- #98 Be a Fred
- #100 Be the Ripple!

Resources:

- **It's Not What Happens in Life, It's What you Do About It** by W. Mitchell – wmitchell.com
- **What's So Amazing About Grace** by Philip Yancey
- **The Furious Longing of God** by Brennan Manning – brennanmanning.com
- Verve in Las Vegas Online Broadcasts – live.mediasocial.tv/ verve

Habit 91

Reclaim and Recycle Your Relationships

"As iron sharpens iron, so one person sharpens another."

– Proverbs 27: 17 (NIV)

What:

I LOVE this habit! Nobody is unsalvageable. Marriages are not disposable and friends are worth investing in. Granted, you don't have to be everyone's friend, but think before you toss someone aside. The quality of relationships are directly proportional to what you invest in them.

Why:

In this day and age, people can simply "unfriend" someone and move on without a second thought. I encourage you to think about it before you do it. If you hit the unfriend button each time you come up against conflict, you might find yourself a bit lacking in conflict resolution skills or perhaps surrounded by a lot of "yes" people. Without throwing stones, "yes" people are people who do not challenge you to raise the bar on who you are.

When we have conflict with others, it can be a golden opportunity to learn something about ourselves as well as how to problem solve. I love to have people in my life I refer to as my "iron" people. These are folks who challenge me to become a better version of myself. While that can be through encouragement, it can also be through healthy criticism by holding a mirror up to me. By pointing out or reflecting my actions or behaviors to me in an uplifting way, I can have an opportunity to become stronger, wiser and just plain a better person.

How To:

The key is twofold: the intention of those individuals you are considering un-friending and your purpose on this planet. If someone is just being mean to be mean and serve some unbeneficial purpose, go directly to the source and discuss it with them from a grounded place. Enlist the help of an arbitrator if necessary. I find more often than not people may say or do hurtful things out of neglect and not being thoughtful rather than sheer evil intentions.

I also have been the perpetrator of jumping to conclusions and assuming someone's intentions. Neither are good; both can many times be resolved through mature problem solving. Granted, if after the discussion there is no resolve, then it becomes a matter of who you are as a person.

Who you are and strive to become has everything to do with how you treat others even if they are being less than who they could be. Are you someone who holds a grudge? Are you someone who is able to forgive? Are you someone who needs forgiveness? Are you a student of grace?

My biggest advice on "How To" Reclaim and Recycle Your Relationships is to become a student of Grace.

Related Healthy Habits:
* #36 Grace
* #95 Social Ministry vs. Social Media

Resources:
* **What's So Amazing About Grace?** by Phillip Yancey
* Author Brennan Manning – brennanmanning.com/publications
* Forgiveness: Letting Go of Grudges and Bitterness from the Mayo Clinic – mayoclinic.com/health/forgiveness/MH00131
* Verve in Las Vegas Online Broadcasts – live.mediasocial.tv/verve

Habit 92

Live Off Balance On Purpose

"Embrace Uncertainty and Create the Life You Love"

– Dan Thurmon

The following contribution is from my friend Dan Thurmon

What:

Living Off Balance On Purpose is about being intentional and committed to what drives you. Instead of hoping that one day you will "achieve balance," embrace life's changes and unpredictability. Perfect balance is unrealistic and, ultimately, undesirable. In fact, you MUST be off balance to learn, grow, and serve others.

Why:

Trying to "achieve balance" will frustrate you. However, if you are connected to a sense of purpose and proactive in the midst of change, you are more available to make a positive contribution to your community. It starts with you, but extends outward to benefit your family, friends, and world.

How To:

- Shed the guilt of not having a "perfectly balanced" life.
- Clarify the purpose that drives you to improve yourself and serve others.
- Embrace the uncertainty you face and initiate positive changes.
- Connect with "what matters most" instead of trying to "compartmentalize" your priorities and time.
- Look for opportunities to support the people and causes you care about.

Thank you, Dan, for your mission, your time and your talent! Thank you for Being a Ripple!

Related Healthy Habits:
- #27 Waking Well
- #41 Be True to Your Quest
- #47 Be Wise With Your Time

Resources:

- **Off Balance on Purpose** by Dan Thurmon – offbalanceonpurpose.com
- Dan Thurmon Keynote Speaker, Author and Work/Life Balance Expert – danthurmon.com

Habit 93

Create A Mastermind Group

What:

"Mastermind groups offer a combination of brainstorming, education, peer accountability and support in a group setting to sharpen your business and personal skills. A mastermind group helps you and your mastermind group members achieve success. Participants challenge each other to set important goals, and more importantly, to accomplish them. The group requires commitment, confidentiality, willingness to be creative and brainstorm ideas/ solutions, and support each other with total honesty, respect and compassion. Mastermind group members act as catalysts for growth, devil's advocates and supportive colleagues. This is the essence and value of mastermind groups." – The Success Alliance

Why:

"As iron sharpens iron, so one person sharpens another." – Proverbs 27: 17 (NIV)

How To:

- Get clarity of self and group intentions before joining or starting a Mastermind group.
- Ask to visit a group as a guest if you have never experienced one before.
- Check out the resources below.
- Create your mission statement if you haven't already and your Strategic Attraction Plan (SAP).
- Focus on actively attracting mastermind group members. Hint: If you are grounding daily and truly working and reading your SAP you will be amazed how this begins to happen.

What a Mastermind group is NOT

- not a networking group
- not group coaching or counseling session
- not a class or seminar

Related Healthy Habits:

- #41 Be True to Your Quest
- #42 Build a Support System
- #47 Be Wise With Your Time
- #67 Be Present While Away

Resources:

- **Books and Recordings** by Napoleon Hill – naphill.org
- **Think and Grow Rich** by Napoleon Hill – naphill.org
- 7 Real-Life Tips for Creating a Successful Mastermind Group_ post by Christine Kane – http://christinekane.com/7-real-life-tips-for-creating-a-successful-mastermind-group
- What is A Mastermind Group? – thesuccessalliance.com/what-is-a-mastermind-group.html

- Master Mind Meetup Groups – mastermind-group.meetup.com
- Strategic Attraction Plan (SAP) Stacey Hall – chi-to-be.com

---

NOTES:

Habit 94

See What Isn't There - Mike Rayburn

What:

Instead of complaining about the world around you, focus on what isn't there by asking yourself, "What If? and Why Not?"

Why:

Complaining about the problems is not the way to find solutions. Complaining about the problems usually only fosters more problems and wastes time and energy. See #48 Focus on the Shoot.

How To:

How do you **See What Isn't There?** Mike Rayburn challenges us to ask "What If?"

What if there were not homeless people in my town? What if I used my time and talent to change lives for the good? What if people in Las Vegas felt a sense of community? What if less fortunate men had a way to share their talent instead of resorting to crime? What if homeless people had socks and didn't have to suffer from the health issues involving chronic foot injuries and infections? Our friend Travis Gluckler (aka: Doc or Brother Jones) asked some of these questions and created a community changing ministry in Sin City he has affectionately called "The Saint City Project."

The second question to ask yourself is "Why Not?" Why not start an after school program for kids? Why not create a project to empower men in the community and utilize their creativity by starting a Street Hip-Hop Record label? Why not do a cross country tour collecting socks for the homeless in Las Vegas?

You don't have to know how you are going to do it right away. Mike also talks about "Writing Music You Can't Play"…yet ;-)

Now your turn...
*What If?

_____

_____

*Why Not?

_____

_____

Related Healthy Habits:
- #48 Focus on the Shoot
- #41 Be True to Your Quest

Resources:

- **What If? Dare to Do More, Be More and Reach Farther Than You Ever Thought Possible** by Mike Rayburn – mikerayburn. com
- Verve in Las Vegas Online Broadcasts – live.mediasocial.tv/verve
- Saint City Project- Dedicated to transforming the city of Las Vegas – saintcityproject.com

Habit 95

Social Ministry vs. Social Media

"If you can't post anything nice, then don't post anything at all. :-)"

Although my mom didn't say this, she would have if there had been internet when I was young. As a kid, if she ever caught me saying something unkind about someone, then I had to say three kind things about them. Great Lesson!

What:

Create and Inspire Social Ministry through your Social Media. Everything you choose to view, post, pin, link to or laugh at has the ability to uplift…or not. Make your Post Count! Seriously, choose to inspire health in your sphere of influence with information, entertainment, resources, laughter and amazing images. Aim to uplift!

Why:

I've seen tragic events occur through mindless or mean public displays of poor energy depletion. When you create or pass on what I call "bad juju," you are not only dragging your energy down but that of those around you as well.

How To:

- Uplift conversations rather than pander or perpetuate bad juju.
- Choose not to feed hate with hate.
- Be Relevant.
- Be Inspirational.
- Find others who are creating Social Ministry and see what they are doing.
- Attract, Support and Propel others creating beneficial thoughts, ideas or images.
- Pray for guidance before posting
- Create the intention for serving others through your posts, pins and pics

Related Healthy Habits:
- #40 Encourage
- #98 Be a Fred

Resources:

- The Healthy Habit Coach – TheHealthyHabitCoach.com
- **100 Easy Healthy Habits: Uplifting Habits for the Mind, Body & Soul** – 100EasyHealthyHabits.com
- Every Resource in this book!
- Facebook for Parents – Linda Fogg Phillips

Habit 96

Envision REAL Health

What:

Discover and visualize what REAL Health is and begin to envision it for yourself. REAL Health is much more than skin deep. REAL Health is attained through sustainable habits rather than fad diets or extreme sports. REAL Health involves the Mind, Body and Soul being powerful, authentic and able to inspire others.

Why:

When we experience REAL Health we have the energy, clarity and inspiration for being the person we were put on this planet to be.

How To:

Ask yourself – What does REAL Health look like to me? Build this image into your daily grounding/goals time and into your Strategic Attraction Plan (SAP).

Related Healthy Habits:
- #2 Manage Your Bucket
- #9 Eat REAL Food
- #37 Create Healthy Boundaries

Resources:

*   Every Resource in this book!

NOTES:

Forgive to Live

"Darkness cannot drive out darkness; only light can do that. Hate cannot drive out hate; only love can do that."

– Martin Luther King, Jr.

"The weak can never forgive. Forgiveness is the attribute of the strong."

– Mahatma Gandhi

What:

"Psychologists generally define forgiveness as a conscious, deliberate decision to release feelings of resentment or vengeance toward a person or group who has harmed you, regardless of whether they actually deserve your forgiveness." – Greater Good, The Science of a Meaningful Life – University of California, Berkley

Why:

"Forgiveness Is the Greatest Healer of Them All. Without

Forgiveness There Is No Future" – Mission of the World Forgiveness Alliance

To be clear…I believe we can practice every healthy habit in this book and still not experience a significant longterm benefit unless we master the habit of "Forgive to Live."

How To:

- Know who you are and why you are here.
- Resolve to Forgive to Live daily.
- Be grateful for forgiveness.
- Become a student of Grace.

Related Healthy Habits:

- #36 Grace
- #91 Reclaim and Recycle Relationships

Resources:

- Dr. Bernie Seigel – berniesiegelmd.com
- Dr. Leo Buscaglia – leobuscaglia.org
- "What is Forgiveness?" Berkeley – greatergood.berkeley.edu/topic/forgiveness/definition
- **What's So Amazing About Grace?** by Phillip Yancey
- Grace Video by U2 – The OGG Blog (Of God's Grace) – ofgodsgrace.blogspot.com/2013/04/grace-makes-beauty-from-ugly-things.html
- What is Forgiveness? by the Mayo Clinic – mayoclinic.com/health/forgiveness/MH00131
- World Forgiveness Alliance – forgivenessday.org (Note: I do not personally know this group but was fascinated by their mission.)

Habit 98

Be a Fred - Mark Sanborn

What:

Fred is a real person, and Fred can be you! Mark Sanborn's Fred books are a fantastic and simple illustration of "how" you do what you do is far more impactful than "what" you do. Okay, so Mark is far more eloquent and explains this principle he derived from observing and getting to know his neighborhood postal carrier, Fred the postman. Fred took excellence seriously and conveyed heartfelt connection to the people on his route. Mark Sanborn shows us how these same principles absolutely apply to successful habits in business and our lives.

Here are the Four Principles of Fred:
- Everyone Makes a Difference
- Everything is Built on Relationships
- You Must Continually Create Value for Others, and it Doesn't Have to Cost a Penny
- You Can Reinvent Yourself Regularly

Why:

Because how you do anything is how you do everything. One person can be a Fred in their community, and create uplifting

Ripples worldwide! Have you seen how many of these books have sold? One man created a ripple that has traveled the world simply by being excellent.

How To:

*   When you have sound mind and a healthy body and soul, you can serve others with effortless and endless energy. Sustainable healthy habits allow us to become a better version of ourselves daily and encourage others to do the same. One ripple can change our world. Imagine what could happen if we all began creating those ripples in our own communities.
*   Be a Fred and Encourage other Freds for their efforts and excellence
*   Live like Fred!

Related Healthy Habits:

*   #1-100

Resources:

*   **Fred Factor** by Mark Sanborn – fredfactor.com
*   **Fred 2.0** by Mark Sanborn – marksanborn.com/fred2/
*   Mark Sanborn – Author, Speaker and Friend of Fred's everywhere – marksanborn.com

Habit 99

Give Gifts of Health

What:

Great uplifting gifts can be free and simple to create. Imagination and creativity can impact lives more than you can imagine. I spent much of my childhood and early adult life struggling financially and found it very difficult not being able to afford to buy presents for my family and friends.

Why:

Because it is not enough to just give for the sake of giving without affecting an uplifting outcome for someone's Mind, Body and Soul.

How To:

- Read **100 Easy Healthy Habits** book and listen to the audio coaching series and GO!
- Look for new book from The Healthy Habit Coach coming in 2014.
- Search Pinterest and Instagram for great ideas.

Related Healthy Habits:
- #77 Share Healthy Habits
- #82 Soup Swap

Resources:

- Look for book from The Healthy Habit Coach coming in 2014 - lifesciencepublishers.com
- The Healthy Habit Coach Blog – Search for the Holiday Gift Series – thehealthyhabitcoach.com/health-and-wellness/20-healthy-holiday-gift-ideas-day-20-merry-christmas/
- Tara Rayburn Pinterest Boards – pinterest.com/tararayburn
- Healthy Habits on Instagram – instagram.com/healthyhabits

Habit 100

Be the Ripple!

What:

When you practice healthy habits, you reflect positive change to the world. The world begins to notice and ask you what you are doing differently. Please share it with them :-D

Why:

"Don't spend your precious time asking, "Why isn't the world a better place?" It will only be time wasted. The question to ask is "How can I make it better?" To that there is an answer." – Dr. Leo Buscaglia

How To:

- Go back to Healthy Habit #1 Simply Start
- Repeat…Often ;-D

Related Healthy Habits:

- #1- 100

Resources:

- The state of your heart
- The state or your relationship with God
- Your willingness to "Be the Ripple!"

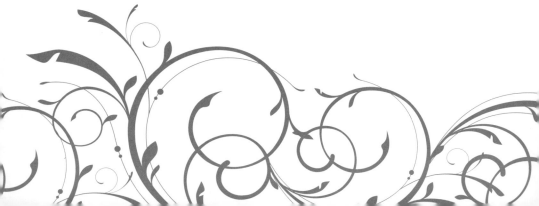

Resources for Life

The Healthy Habit Coach Resources:

- The Healthy Habit Coach – thehealthyhabitcoach.com
- Tara@theHealthyHabitCoach.com
- Blog – thehealthyhabitcoach.com/blog
- LinkedIn – linkedin.com/in/tararayburn
- Twitter – twitter.com/TaraRayburn
- Facebook – facebook.com/thehealthyhabitcoach
- Google+ – plus.google.com - Tara Rayburn
- Pinterest – pinterest.com/tararayburn
- Instagram – instagram.com/healthyhabits
- The OGG Blog – Of God's Grace – ofgodsgrace.blogspot.com
- Juice Plus+ supplements – thehealthyhabitcoach.com/store
- Young Living Essential Oils store – abundanceandwisdom. com/tararayburn or youngliving.org/tararayburn
- Young Living distributor ID# 866847 NOTE: If you are a Young Living distributor or already working with a distributor or upline please continue working with them.

Books by Tara Rayburn:

- Available from Life Science Publishing – lifesciencepublishers.com and Amazon.com
- **100 Easy Healthy Habits** by Tara Rayburn – 100EasyHealthyHabits.com
- **Essential Gluten-Free Recipes 2nd Edition** – by Tara Rayburn and Mary Vars
- Essential Gluten-Free Recipes on Facebook – facebook.com/ pages/Essential-Gluten-Free-Recipes

Mary the Mentor Mom Resources:

- Ms. Mary's Cooking Website – msmaryscooking.com
- e-mail – mkvars@verizon.net
- Ms. Mary's Cooking on Facebook – facebook.com/groups/207451485962346

Information & Education

- Weston A. Price Foundation – westonaprice.org
- Wise Traditions annual conferences and journals – westonaprice.org
- Wise Traditions conference recordings – fleetwoodonsite.com
- Price-Pottenger Nutrition Foundation – ppnf.org
- Dr. Mary Enig, expert on fats & oils – coconutoil.com
- Dr. Kaayla Daniel – drkaayladaniel.com
- Dr. Joseph Mercola – mercola.com
- Dr. Natasha Campbell-McBride – guthealth.com and putyourhearinyourmouth.com
- Alana Sugar, CN. certified nutritionist/whole food consultant – alanasugar.com
- Donna Gates – Body Ecology – bodyecology.com
- Farm-to-Consumer Legal Defense Fund – protecting farms, farmers and REAL food access – farmtoconsumer.org
- Environmental Working Group – the power of information – ewg.org
- Jeffrey M. Smith – world GMO expert and author – responsibletechnology.org
- Nourishing Our Children – resources for teaching the importance of nutrient-rich diets – nourishingourchildren.org
- Stacey Hall – Saving the lives of people stressed to the snapping point! – chi-to-be.com

Holistic/Integrative Health Specialists

- The Nevada Clinic, Integrative Medicine for Health and Wellness, NV – nevadaclinic.com
- Hetzel Chiropractic – Dr. David Hetzel, NV – 702-260-1164
- Dr. Michael Bell DDS – Bell Center for Holistic Dentistry – lvtmjdentist.com
- Hilgartner Chiropractic and Nutrition Consulting – Dr. Pete and Lolin Hilgartner. VA – hilgartnerhealth.com
- Loudoun Holistic Partners – Anne Stewart, MD, David Stewart, MD – loudounholistichealthpartners.com
- Kaayla T. Daniel, PhD – nutrition consultant, NM – drkaayladaniel.com, wholesoystory.com
- Alana Sugar, CN. certified nutritionist and whole food consultant – alanasugar.com
- Joette Calabrese – Homeopathy – joettecalabrese.com

Resources for REAL Health, Exercise & Information

- Environmental Working Group – ewg.org
- Dr. Masaru Emoto -masaru-emoto.net
- OxyCise – Deep Breathing and gentle isometrics – oxycise.com
- Breathing Exercises – drweil.com
- Dr. Pete Hilgartner – The Hilgartner Health Institute – HilgartnerHealth.com
- Pilates Master Aliesa George – Centerworks Functional Fitness – centerworks.com
- The Nia Technique – nianow.com
- Urban Zen – urbanzen.org
- Nutritionist Dr. Lolin Hilgartner – hilgartnerhealth.com
- PX90 – home exercise program – beachbody.com

- Qi Gong – Google resources online of find a local class
- Wellness Travel and Spa Finder – spafinder.com

Nutrition, Health, Blogs & Online Communities

- Tara Rayburn – thehealthyhabitcoach.com
- Healthy Habits Meetup Group – meetup.com/ HealthyHabitsLasVegas
- Village Green Network – villagegreennetwork.com
- Kelly the Kitchen Kop – kellythekitchenkop.com
- The Healthy Home Economist – thehealthyhomeeconomist. com
- CheeseSlave – cheeseslave.com
- Stacey Hall and the Chi-To-Be books, audios and movement – chi-to-be.com
- Matt Stone – author/independent health researcher – 180degreehealth.com
- Caroline Lunger – mygutsy.com
- Dr. Joseph Mercola – mercola.com
- Two Angry Moms – angrymoms.org
- Laura Waldo – livingglutenandgrainfree.com
- Dhyana Center – dhyanacenter.com
- Joette Calabrese – Homeopathy – joettecalabrese.com
- Nourishing Our Children blog – REAL food topics for REAL health – nourishingourchildren.wordpress.com
- Verve in Las Vegas Online Broadcasts – live.mediasocial.tv/ verve
- Meetup.com – Online message board for local community interest groups
- Kimberly Hartke – real food blogger/activist – hartkeisonline. com
- Butter Buddies of Weston A. Price – community.westonaprice.

org
- The Entrepreneur's Source Blog – entrepreneurssource.com/blog.html

Chefs, Farms and REAL Food Resources

- Find your local farmers' market – farm-fresh pastured eggs – localharvest.org
- APP Farmer's Market Locator – itunes.apple.com/us/app/farmers-market-locator
- Green Pasture – fermented cod liver oil, butter oil – greenpasture.org
- Eat Wild – directory for grass-fed food and facts – eatwild.com
- Soaking, sprouting and fermenting grains – westonaprice.org
- Chef Shane Kelly – chefshanekelly.com
- Weston A. Price Foundation Chapter Leaders – westonaprice.org/local-chapters/find-local-chapter
- Monica Corrado – Simply Being Well – simplybeingwell.com
- Nourishing Our Children – resources for teaching the importance of nutrient-rich diets – nourishingourchildren.org
- Bloomin' Desert Herb Farm – bloomindesertherbs.com
- Mountain Rose Herbs – for bulk herbs and herbal teas – mountainroseherbs.com
- Chef Pete Ghione – recipes for life – cancercuisine.com
- Fields of Athenry Farm, VA – fieldsofathenryfarm.com
- Quail Hollow Farm, NV – quailhollowfarmcsa.com
- Bloomin' Desert Herb Farm, NV – 702-301-8996
- Herbal Experience – herbalexperience.net
- Coconut Wate Kefir – Body Ecology – bodyecology.com
- The Las Vegas Farm – thelasvegasfarm.com
- Dr. OhHira's Probiotics – vitacost.com
- PRObiotic 225 by Ortho Molecular Products

- Bar 10 Beef – bar10beef.com
- Polyface Farm – Joel Salatin – polyfacefarms.com
- China Ranch Date Farm, CA – Dates, hiking and fun – Chinaranch.com
- Vital Choice – wild salmon – vitalchoice.com
- Green Pasture – Fermented Cod Liver Oil – greenpasture.org
- Digestive Enzyme Supplements – Young Living – youngliving. com or Enzymedica – enzymedica.com
- Spectrum – coconut, palm, olive oil – spectrumorganics.com
- Tropical Traditions – coconut oil – tropicaltraditions.com
- Dried NingXia wolfberries – youngliving.org/tararayburn
- Freeland Foods – sprouted seeds and quinoa – goraw.com
- Crystallized ginger – gingerpeople.com
- Natural Zing – organic, raw, living foods – naturalzing.com
- Raw Makery – live, organic, and sprouted breads, crackers, and cookies – rawmakery.com
- Go Raw Cafe & Juice Bar – gorawcafe.com

Essential Oil Resources

***IMPORTANT: Know your farmer and their ethics. Do not purchase cheap oils. Cheap oils get cheap results – or worse. Trust me; I speak from very painful experience.

If you already work with a Young Living Distributor or heard about Young Living from someone please honor them by contacting that person for orders and resources.

If you would like to become a distributor or place an order go to: Young Living Essential Oils – youngliving.org/tararayburn or abundanceandwisdom.com/tararayburn

- Kitchen essential oil caddies and displays – Jeff Toleson – TheraPure.com
- Essential Oil Cool Mist Diffusers – diffuserworld.com/735. html for discount on diffuser purchase use coupon code: A735SAVE5
- Online essential oils testimonials – share what you know, learn what you don't know – oil-testimonials.com
- Essential Oils Travel cases – Abundant Health – abundanthealth4u.com
- Castor Oil from The Heritage Store – heritagestore.com or BAAR – baar.com
- Kukui Oil from Oils of Aloha – oilsofaloha.com
- **Essential Oils Desk Reference** – lifesciencepublishers.com
- **Essential Oils Pocket Reference** – lifesciencepublishers. com
- **The Chemistry of Essential Oils Made Easy** by Dr. David Stewart
- **The Animal Desk Reference** by Melissa Shelton DVM
- **Essential Gluten-Free Recipes: Simple, Nutrient Rich, Essential Oil Infused** – lifesciencepublishers.com

Gluten-Free Food Resources

- Tru Roots – organic, sprouted rice, seeds and quinoa – truroots.com
- To Your Health Sprouted Flour Co – gluten-free flours and more – organicsproutedflour.net
- The Raw Food World Store – sprouted chia/flax crackers – therawfoodworld.com
- Sprouted crackers and chips – REAL, live food – goraw.com
- Namaste Foods – gluten-free, allergy-friendly mixes – namastefoods.com

- Sami's Bakery – millet flax bread, crackers and wraps – samisbakery.com
- Bob's Red Mill – gluten-free oats and flours – bobsredmill.com/gluten-free
- Grindstone Bakery – wheat-free, gluten-free, "soaked" breads – grindstonebakery.com
- Lydia's Organics – gluten-free/nut-free granola – lydiasorganics.com
- Enjoy Life Foods – gluten-free/nut-free granola – enjoylifefoods.com
- Dr. Natasha Campbell-McBride – GAPS Diet resources – gapsdiet.com

Books/Reading List

- **100 Easy Healthy Habits: Uplifting Habits for the Mind, Body and Soul** – Audio coaching series and book by Tara Rayburn
- **The Complete Master Cleanse and Beyond the Master Cleanse** by Tom Woloshyn – themastercleanse.org
- **The Bible** by God :-D
- **Earthly Bodies and Heavenly Hair** by Dina Falconi
- **How to Feel 10 Years Younger in 90 days or Less** by Dr. Pete Hilgartner, hilgartnerhealth.com
- **Healthy Healing** by Linda Page, Ph.D
- **The Whole Soy Story** by Dr. Kaayla Daniel
- **Flash Foresight** by Dan Burrus – burrus.com
- **Nourishing Traditions** by Sally Fallon Morell and Mary Enig
- **Put Your Heart in Your Mouth** by Dr. Natasha Campbell-McBride
- **Gut and Psychology Syndrome** by Dr. Natasha Campbell-McBride

- **The Daniel Fast** by Susan Gregory – daniel-fast.com
- **Cure Tooth Decay: Remineralize Cavities and Repair Your Teeth Naturally** by Ramiel Nagel
- **Essential Oil Desk Reference** published by Life Science Publishing
- **Essential Oils Pocket Reference** – lifesciencepublishers. com
- **Seeds of Deception and Genetic Roulette** by Jeffery Smith
- **Chi-To-Be! Achieving Your Ultimate B-All** by Stacey Hall
- **Attracting the Perfect Customer** by Stacey Hall and Jan Brogniez
- **The Unhealthy Truth** by Robyn O'Brien
- **The Artist's Way** by Julia Cameron
- **Body Ecology Diet** by Donna Gates
- **30 Ways to Help in Helpless Situations** by Rob Payne – robscolumns.wordpress.com
- **The Liver and GallBladder Miracle Cleanse** by Andreas Moritz
- **Healing Childhood Ear Infections** by Dr. Michael A. Schmidt
- **Beauty by God** by Shelly Ballestero
- **Jesus Calling** by Sarah Young is a great devotional
- **Nature's Mold Rx** by Edward and Jacquelyn Close
- **The Animal Desk Reference** by Melissa Shelton DVM
- **The Chemistry of Essential Oils Made Easy** by Dr. David Stewart
- Anything written by Dr. David Stewart ;-)
- **Think and Grow Rich** by Napoleon Hill – naphill.org
- **The Success Principles** by Jack Canfield – jackcanfield.com
- **Chicken Soup for the Soul Series** coauthored by Jack Canfield
- **What If? Dare to Do More, Be More and Reach Farther Than**

You Ever Thought Possible by Mike Rayburn – mikerayburn. com
- **Off Balance on Purpose** by Dan Thurmon – offbalanceonpurpose.com
- **Fred Factor** by Mark Sanborn – fredfactor.com
- **Fred 2.0** by Mark Sanborn – marksanborn.com/fred2/
- 1001 Uses for White Distilled Vinegar – vinegartips.com
- **What's So Amazing About Grace?** by Phillip Yancey
- Author Brennan Manning – brennanmanning.com/publications

Personal Success, Faith and Inspiration

- Dan Burrus – technology trends and wisdom – burrus.com
- Jack Canfield – jackcanfield.com
- **Attracting the Perfect Customers** by Stacey Hall and Jan Brogniez
- Brian Tracy for goal setting and success – briantracy.com
- **What If?** by Mike Rayburn – Keynote Artist, Author, Guitar Virtuoso – MikeRayburn.com
- **The Bible** by God :-D
- **Jesus Calling** by Sarah Young is a great devotional
- **The Artist's Way** by Julia Cameron
- **Off Balance, On Purpose** by Dan Thurmon
- The Secret – jackcanfield.com
- The Keeper of the Keys – jackcanfield.com
- Tapping – jackcanfield.com
- **The Time is Now, The Person is You** by Nido Qubein
- **Do It Well. Make It Fun** by Ronald P. Culberson
- **Flash Foresight** by Dan Burrus – burrus.com
- **Embracing the Grey: A Wing, A Prayer and a Doubters Resolve** by Mark Hollingsworth
- Verve Broadcasts Online – vimeo.com/channels/watchverve

- **The Road Less Traveled** by M. Scott Peck
- **Renegade and Guerilla Lovers** by Vince Antonucci
- **What's So Amazing About Grace?** by Phillip Yancey
- Philip Yancey's blog – philipyancey.com/q-and-a-topics/grace
- **The Ragamuffin Gospel** and **The Furious Longing of God** by Brennan Manning
- **The Life You've Always Wanted** by John Ortberg
- **The Different Drum: Community and Making Peace** by M. Scott Peck – mscottpeck.com
- **Fred Factor** and **Fred 2.0** by Mark Sanborn – marksanborn. com
- **Married for Life** by David C. Cook
- **Chi-To-Be** book, audio series and coaching By Stacey Hall – chi-to-be.com
- **Overcoming Cancer: A Journey of Faith** by Judi Moreo – judimoreo.com
- Dr. Leo Buscaglia – buscaglia.com
- Dr. Bernie Seigel – berniesiegelmd.com
- **The Purpose Driven Life** by Rick Warren

Philanthropy

These are projects personally recommended by The Healthy Habit Coach:

- The SaintCity Project – saintcityproject.com
- The Cupcake Girls (Las Vegas/Portland) – thecupcakegirls.org
- Verve Church in Vegas – vivalaverve.org
- Team Focus – Supporting boys without fathers in their lives – teamfocususa.org
- Compassion International – Child Sponsorship – compassion. com

- Willow Creek Association Church in your area – willowcreek. com/membership
- Tatto Church – Tattoers Helping Tattoers in Need – tattoochurch. com
- The Shade Tree Shelter – Emergency Shelter for woman and children in Las Vegas – theshadetree.org
- Noah's Animal House – Providing shelter for the animals of women and children in The Shade Tree shelter in Las Vegas – noahsanimalhouse.org
- Dress for Success – dressforsuccess.org
- Orphan Network – Sponsor children in Nicaragua – Orphan Network - orphanetwork.org
- Prison Entrepreneurship Program – Changing the Future by Recycling the Past for inmates and their families – prisonentrepreneurship.org

Essential Tools & Equipment

- Vitacost Online is a resource for many of your health supporting items – vitacost.com
- Excalibur Dehydrator – excaliburdehydrator.com
- Kids Konserve – waste-free lunch packing for the whole family – kidskonserve.com
- Natural Value – unbleached wax paper
- Le Crueset – cookware – lecreuset.com
- Yonanas Maker – soft-serve frozen fruit snack maker – yonanas.com
- Tovolo – non toxic popsicle-making molds – tovolo.com
- Stainless steel popsicle molds – lifewithoutplastic.com/ freezycup
- Joyce Chen's Bamboo 3-pc Steamer – Bed, Bath and Beyond
- Young Living – titanium cooking pots, pans and glass steamers

– youngliving.org/tararayburn
- Nourishing Our Children – nourishingourchildren.org
- Canning Jar Drinking glasses – jarstore.com
- Nubius- stainless steel containers and lunch boxes – nubiusorganics.com
- Lifefactory – glass water bottles for adults, children and babies – lifefactory.com
- Essential oils kitchen caddies & stands – Jeff Toleson – TheraPure.com
- Silicone molds and pans – Wilton – wilton.com or available at Michael's
- Baraka Ceramic Net Pots – sinussupport.com
- Cool Mist Diffusers – DiffuserWorld.com – For a discount code A735SAVE5
- Castor Oil from The Heritage Store – heritagestore.com or BAAR – baar.com
- Glass spray bottles available from – abundanthealth4u.com

GMO Education, Action, Safe Products and Vendors

- Genetic Roulette – the Movie – geneticroulettemovie.com
- Jeffery Smith, The Institute for Responsible Technology – responsibletechnology.org
- The Non-Gmo Project – nongmoproject.org
- Non-GMO Shopping Guide and APP – nongmoshoppingguide.com
- Price-Pottenger Nutrition Foundation – ppnf.org
- The Weston A. Price Foundation – westonaprice.org
- The Weston A. Price Shopping Guide – westonaprice.org
- Nourishing Our Children – nourishingourchildren.org
- Environmental Working Group – EWG.org

- Body Ecology – Donna Gates – bodyecology.com
- Bloomin' Desert Herb Farm – bloomindesertherbs.com
- Dr. OhHira's Professional Formula Probiotics – harvestmoonhealthfoods.com
- PRObiotic 225 from Ortho Molecular Products
- Juice Plus+ Whole Food Supplements – Order from thehealthyhabitcoach.com/blog

Places, Ideas and Sites to Get Curious About

- Teach Them to Fish Foundation – teachthemtofish.org
- Nourishing Our Children – nourishingourchildren.org
- Price-Pottenger Nutrition Foundation – ppnf.org
- Weston A. Price Foundation Chapter Leaders – westonaprice.org/local-chapters/find-local-chapter
- Tapping – jackcanfield.com
- Coconut Oil Pulling and Research – coconutresearchcenter.org
- Wise Tradition Conference DVD's and CD's – fleetwoodonsite.com
- Blessing Ranch/Blessing Bay – Dr. John Walker, Dr. Charity Walker and Deanna Walker – blessingranch.org

Gratitude

**"With man this is impossible, but with God
all things are possible."**

– Matthew 19: 26

First of all, I give thanks Jesus Christ, without whom any of my endeavors would be possible.Ad eius gloriam! To His Glory!

Special Thank You:
Thank You to Pearl Koplinski, Marian Howcroft and Evelyn Crandall – you inspired my love for health as a child. Thank You to my amazing husband, Mike Rayburn for holding my hand on the mountain top. Thank You to Seneca and Zachary Rayburn for all of your patience, courage and laughter along the way. Thank You to Kim and Joe Caro for your grace, character and strength while on a difficult journey. Thank You to Mary Vars for your friendship, wisdom, faith and friendship.

Ongoing Gratitude:
Thank You to Troie Battles and Life Science Publishing for your belief in my work. Thank You Gary and Mary Young for Young Living Essential Oils, and to my Young Living Oil's family around the globe. Thank You to Stacey Hall for your friendship, coaching and heart for uplifting our world through Chi-To-Be and it's worldwide family.

Thank You Verve Church in Las Vegas, for the opportunity to grow my faith and serve alongside the most amazing people. Thank You to My Micro and Macro Groups, your support is priceless. Thank You to all the lives surrounding the work of The Cupcake Girls in Las Vegas – You Are Ripples!

Thank You Dr. Weston A. Price and Francis M. Pottenger for your valuable work during your lives. Thank You to Sally Fallon Morell, Mary Enig and Dr. Kaayla Daniel. Thank You to Jeffery Smith and the folks at the Non GMO Project for your important work. Thank You to Donna Gates of Body Ecology and Dr. Natasha Campbell-McBride. Thank You to all of my Foodie Friends for sharing recipes, laughter, tears and being Ripples of Health in our world.

Great Thanks to my farmer friends, Elaine Boland – Fields of Athenry Farm. Laura and Monte Bledsoe – Quail Hollow Farm. Sharon Linsenbardt – The Las Vegas Farm. You transform our world through your missions.

Thank You to Dr. Pete and Lolin Hilgartner and Dr. Anne and Dr. David Stewart. Thank You to The Nevada Wellness Clinic, Dr. Michael Bell and his team in Las Vegas, Dr. David Hetzel and Dr. Sudir Kapila for your holistic excellence. Thank you Dr. John and Deanna Walker at Blessing Ranch/Blessing Bay for creating a space for God to work.

Thank You to Sharon and Dan Burrus for providing the wonderful reason to be in Maui which created the inspiration for this book. Thank You Jack Canfield for your wonderful endorsement and your support for this project. Thank You to all of my friends in Speakers Roundtable and the National Speakers Association for being Ripples throughout the world. Thank You to the Khazeni Family for being a part of our village and loving our family.

Extra Special Thanks to:
All of you who are uplifting your lives and keeping this mission of Healthy Habits in your hearts and prayers.

About the Author

Tara Rayburn, The Healthy Habit Coach, is an author, speaker, blogger and a Mom-on-a-Mission. Her mission is inspiring uplifting habits for the mind, body and soul. Tara truly believes that the best health care plan is to simply care for your health. She also believes that your daily habits contribute more to your quality of life than any fad diets, exercise craze or magic pill.

Tara shares simple habits for infusing nutrient rich foods, essential oils and old world wisdom into today's busy lifestyle. Her first book Essential Gluten-Free Recipes 2nd Edition is coauthored with Mary Vars and a great resource for REAL food recipes and is also available from Life Science Publishing.

Tara lives in Las Vegas where she enjoys being a wife, a mother of two and friend in her community. Some of her additional passions are volunteering with The Cupcake Girls in Las Vegas and serving as a Weston A. Price Foundation Chapter leader. She loves creating community alongside her friends at Verve Church in Las Vegas, a town where some say there is no community – vivalaverve.org

You can check in with her for ongoing news and resources at TheHealthyHabitCoach.com

* SPEAKER

* AUTHOR

* BLOGGER

* BREAKOUT

SESSIONS

* MOM-ON-A-MISSION

theHealthyHabitCoach.com

What If...?
* Keynote Artist
* Books
* CD's
MIKE RAYBURN
MIKERAYBURN.COM

"A cheerful heart is good medicine."

- Proverbs 17: 22 NLT

"For beautiful eyes,
look for the good in others;
for beautiful lips, speak only words of kindness;
and for poise, walk with the knowledge
that you are never alone."

- Audrey Hepburn

Partner with The Cupcake Girls to create
Ripples of Health in the lives of women
in the adult entertainment industry.

TheCupcakeGirls.org

Church for people who don't like church

7850 S. Dean Martin Drive, Suite 503
Las Vegas, Nevada

"Diseases of the soul are more dangerous and more numerous than those of the body."

- Cicero

*"An Agent of Lifestyle Change
Disguised as a Recipe Book."*

- Mike Rayburn, CSP, CPAE

ESSENTIAL
GLUTEN-FREE RECIPES
SIMPLE * NUTRIENT RICH * ESSENTIAL OIL INFUSED

LIFE SCIENCE PUBLISHING

Available at
LifeSciencePublishers.com

BY TARA RAYBURN & MARY VARS

"A good laugh and a long sleep are the best cures in the doctor's book."

- Irish Proverb